Will America Self-Destruct?

Will America Self-Destruct?

Walter H. Stern

Writers Club Press
San Jose New York Lincoln Shanghai

Will America Self-Destruct?

All Rights Reserved © 2001 by Walter H. Stern

No part of this book may be reproduced or transmitted in any form or by any means, graphic, electronic, or mechanical, including photocopying, recording, taping, or by any information storage or retrieval system, without the permission in writing from the publisher.

Writers Club Press
an imprint of iUniverse.com, Inc.

For information address:
iUniverse.com, Inc.
5220 S 16th, Ste. 200
Lincoln, NE 68512
www.iuniverse.com

ISBN: 0-595-16449-8

Printed in the United States of America

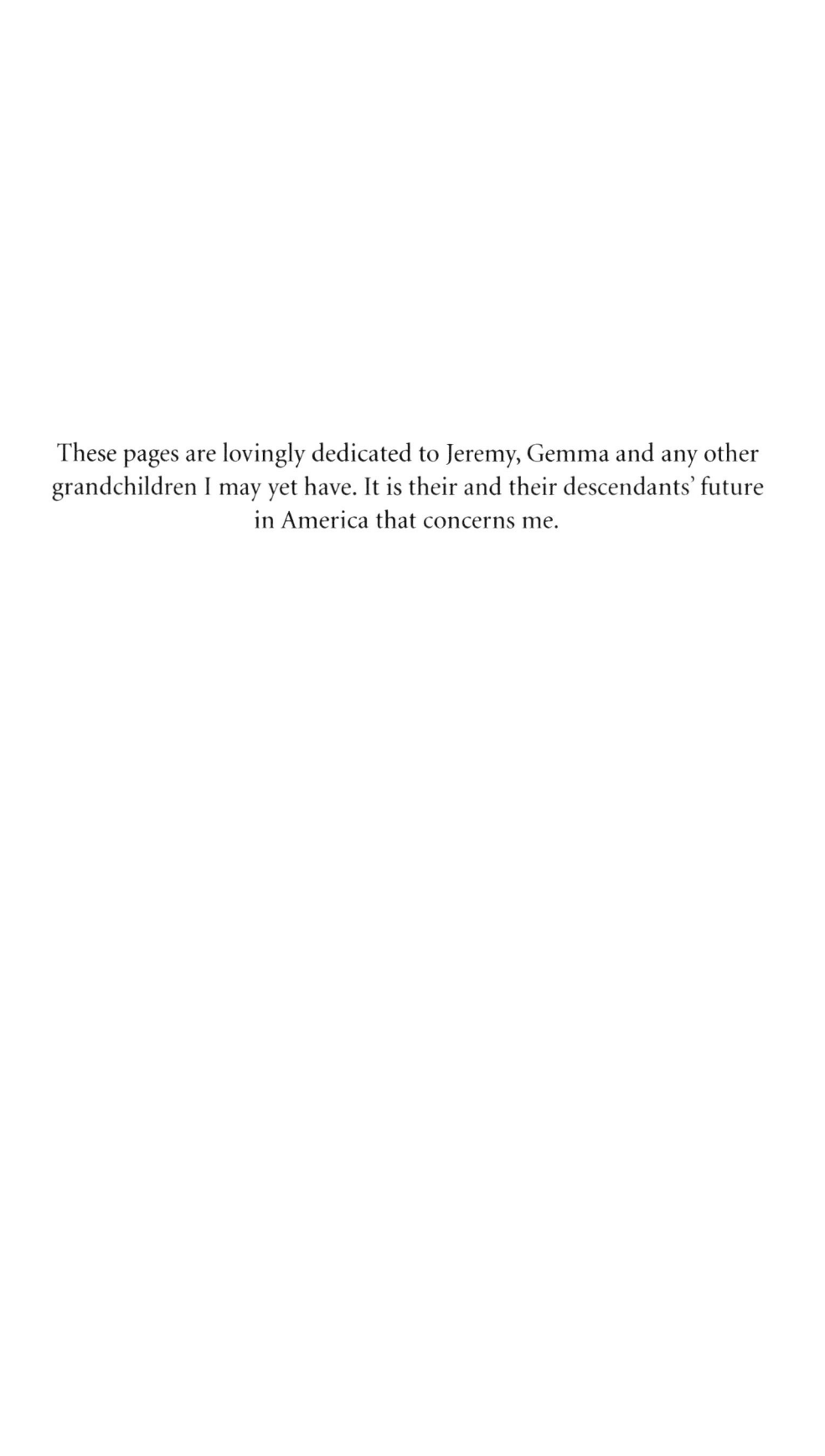

These pages are lovingly dedicated to Jeremy, Gemma and any other grandchildren I may yet have. It is their and their descendants' future in America that concerns me.

Preface

I love the country that adopted me; not only adopted me with open arms at a time of great peril, but fulfilled the American dream for me, though nothing on my part entitled me to its great promise. To contemplate, as I do here, the potential downfall of this great nation may seem churlish at best, rooted perhaps in some personal disappointment or frustration. I propose to do nothing of the sort.

Rather, I am concerned that, for all its solid institutions and safeguards, the United States may have trolleyed off on a tangential track, propelled by the combined forces of desirable pluralism run amok. Taken individually, these special interests may be laudable and even justified. Together, they produce a diversion so intractable that the real goals of the American way of life become blurred in a cloud of confusion, acrimony, and indecision. This has happened before in history—in current and in earlier civilizations. Like an incipient illness, this disintegration is treatable through early diagnosis and corrective treatment. These pages, therefore, are intended to be diagnostic and hopefully curative, rather than critical or rooted in despair. Nothing in this country's history would indicate that the United States is incapable of a course correction when its institutions have gone astray or timely repairs when adversity or normal wear and tear have torn its national fabric.

Having said that, however, there are signs that some of our best intentions as individuals or organizations may have misfired. We hear and read the praises of pluralism and, in the next breath, denunciations of special interests. Are they not one and the same? The awakening to the need for preserving the environment is a case in point. Quite aside from general agreement that environmental protection has become a critical issue, we splinter off into special interests concerned with different priorities or conflicting approaches to a solution. Is this pluralism or something more sinister? The apparent solution to a specific ecological problem in the minds of some may well pose a new, different and equally serious problem for others. What is true of environmental decisions can also be said of economic policy, social programs or virtually anything else to which a democratic government is expected to respond. Those who feel entitled to express their opinions on such matters base their entitlement on pluralism. They look upon those who disagree as special interests.

The glib answer to this dichotomy is the hackneyed "That's what makes horse racing," or, more to the point, "Everybody is entitled to his opinion." True enough, but a democratic government is a highly sensitive instrument that responds to every tick like a seismograph. In the process, constituencies become distorted, policies skewed, and the democratic process perverted.

But government is neither at the root of the problem nor solely responsible for its solution. That responsibility rests with the people, to whose demands government ultimately responds in a free society. There are those who demand that government do for them what, for a variety of reasons, they cannot or will not do for themselves. Some among them believe that government has evolved into an all-inclusive service industry that must cater to all factions of the electorate. A more practical sector of this group holds that the people pay the taxes that fund government operations and that they want only what they are paying for. And yet, within this group it is easy to find people who concede that government is by no means the most efficient provider of these services.

There is yet another faction; one that believes quite sincerely that government is a creation of the people and owes them an obligation of service in a variety of human needs. Their position is founded on the belief that the individual's problem becomes a national problem in that no one among us is unique. In a sense, this may be true, but carrying this theory to its ultimate conclusion, Washington and the other seats of government become supermarkets where the taxpayer redeems his marker for money he has already paid.

The growth of our bureaucracy attests to this. There is no sense in railing against the size of government when we, ourselves, demand that the public apparatus do for us what we should either do for ourselves or obtain from a provider in the private sector.

Worse still, it places the public servant in a quandary from the day he attains public office. Having catered to his constituency's whims to get elected, he now has to engage in the delicate balancing act of redeeming his promises, conforming to his political party's precepts and, most difficult of all, making peace with his own conscience and intellectual dictates. No wonder, then, that this dilemma turns less stouthearted office-holders to the cynicism of acting in their own best interests—getting reelected, aspiring to still higher office or, in some cases, feathering their nests for the day their constituents turn them out at the polls.

All of this is the inevitable result of an abdication by people from such basic tasks as making choices, taking risks and owning up to responsibility. This may sound callous in light of the deprivation suffered by an appreciable segment of our society—people not sufficiently educated to make choices, ill-equipped to take risks, and too poor to afford responsibility for their acts. We, as a people, bear an obligation toward our less fortunate neighbors. And perhaps it makes sense to delegate the discharge of that obligation to various agencies of government, but we pay a price for government's assumption of this responsibility. We all agree that safe, comfortable housing should be a birthright of every family, regardless of ability to pay. But how many among us understand the ins and outs of the many government programs that subsidize rents, guarantee mortgages or provide shelter in various ways? How, then, can we detect malfeasance in these programs until it erupts into a major scandal? Still, we are outraged when these carefully contrived programs fail to accomplish their mission of housing the poor. Much the same can be said of many well-intentioned ventures of the public sector.

One of these that troubles us most is our moral obligation to vouchsafe health care for everyone. The simple procedure of visiting a physician for an affordable fee has given way to an intricate system of third-party insurers, health maintenance organizations of private or semi-private provenance, not to mention the government itself. With pharmaceutical prices constantly on the rise, we find ourselves in a quandary when it comes to assuring everyone, especially the elderly and poor, that they can obtain what the doctor prescribes at a cost they can afford. Typically, what should be a searching debate for finding solutions is degenerating into a flurry of recriminations and investigations that leave the needy patient not much better off than he was before.

There are those who praise the media's role in bringing chicanery to light. And there are those who damn the media for muckraking. There is an element that views the media as the surrogate of the people. But, by definition, a surrogate is someone who acts on behalf of the incompetent and the dead. We need to be informed, and we need to know the opinions of others in order to make our own judgments. What we do not need is someone to chew our intellectual food for us before spooning it into our mouths. There is, of course, the argument that in our complex world we cannot be experts on every subject and need consultants, as it were, to digest data for our consumption, a role we have allowed the media to assume. However, if we follow this course, we can never be sure that the views presented to us have validity or sincerity. The fact that most media follow the course of integrity does not spare us from being victimized by the few that ply their own agenda.

In the final analysis, our well-being is our own responsibility. If that offends the disadvantaged, let me hasten to add that we cannot enjoy our own well-being if we turn our backs on and fail to share with those who are hard-put to fend for themselves. But if we collectively shirk responsibility for making life secure, enriching and rewarding, disintegration of our society is sure to ensue. The fabric that the Founding Fathers so carefully stitched together will come apart at the seams, and the task of mending it will be Herculean. A stitch in time is what this book is all about.

MAKING CHOICES I

Making choices is one of the indispensable disciplines of human existence. Those who master it tend to succeed. This is true of nations as well as of individuals. A look back into history tells us that the great men and women of their time—leaders, discoverers, statesmen—were distinguished for their ability to make choices; difficult choices, unpopular ones, heroic and even fatal choices. What distinguished them from the rest of us is their ability to translate the process of choosing into epic proportions. When we, as a nation, lose the capacity to choose, we relinquish our grasp on destiny and drift into oblivion.

Choices are not made in a vacuum, nor should they be. We seek advice, we welcome influence, and we need support for our decisions from those considered knowledgeable and whose loyalty to our causes we do not question, thus arriving at some degree of consensus. There is value in consensus because it represents parallel thinking and compatible choices by groups with similar objectives and faced with common problems. It does not mean that one person made a choice and others followed sheeplike in order to avoid making choices of their own. To support another's decision must be a choice in itself.

Choice can be equated with will because a choice becomes meaningless if it lacks conviction and the determination to implement it. I am often amused by phantom horse players who make imaginary bets and calculate their would-be winnings on paper, or those who relish gains they would have made in the stock market had they actually bought the securities they followed. Not that I would encourage reckless gambling. Rather, I am inclined to ask why it is that, having been so certain of their choices, these people did not put their money where their pencils pointed. The answer is clear: the courage of their convictions was stripped away by the reality of risk.

Choices do entail risks. But the risks of shirking choices are far greater. They preclude success as well as failure. And while failure is to be avoided, it is an inevitable ingredient of achieving the objectives we equate with success. Rarely has an enviable career been studded with a series of successes without a sprinkling of disappointments and reverses as well. This is proof that choices were made. Much the same is true of nations. Nations are nothing more than amalgams of the personae that inhabit them. Civilizations in decline are those that have lost their decisiveness either through internal strife or through a lack of will brought on by smug reliance on the ramparts built by their forebears. It is a stage of disdevelopment that sneaks up on nations and civilizations and, before its perniciousness can be stemmed, sends them on the path to decline. It is this stage that the United States currently faces, though still incipient and not beyond retrieve.

Why else are we still divided on the ultimate punishment for the most heinous crimes? Why do we hide behind litigiousness as a substitute for solving problems rationally? Why do we still tolerate prejudice and injustice? Where is our resolve to live within our means? The inescapable answer is that we have failed to summon up the courage to face critical choices and the agonies they involve.

Nothing is more agonizing than the contemplation of someone's death at our hands. Our uneasiness with it has been reinforced periodically by wars after which those who served still recoil at the abandon with which they killed. Their consciences are salved by the knowledge that the cause was just and that, more often than not, they were saving their own lives in the act. Perhaps more than any civilization before us, we treasure the sanctity of life and disdain the prospect of institutionalized execution. But precisely because we prize human lives so highly, we ought not to shy away from death as the severest penalty the state can inflict. Because it is irreversible? In the mind of the wrongdoer, it is more to be avoided than any other punishment. To this extent, at least, it serves as a deterrent to crime, though statistics could me marshaled to persuade us otherwise. As things stand now, our penal code provides every possible safeguard against the death penalty's misuse –provisions for homicides committed in self-defense or by incompetents, or in the guise of euthanasia. Current law also guards against misjudgments through an almost infinite series of appeals that mock the state's resolve to carry out the sentence and, ironically, inflict compounded torture on the condemned by keeping them on death row interminably.

Our reluctance to make the choice seems not to stem from humanitarian motives, because the justly condemned deserve no humane consideration. Rather it signifies an aversion to violence, albeit carefully controlled violence. Those who object articulately to the death penalty may well have right on their side and, perhaps, we should accede to their arguments. Once we have made that election, however, we must also live with the risks. We will have forfeited the privilege of clamoring when innocent victims are gunned down in our streets by criminals who do not fear mere incarceration and its flabby system of parole and probation. But a choice has to be made.

Sometimes our inability to make choices results from procrastination. For nearly six decades we have been warned that the world's reserves of hydrocarbons are finite, and that we must prepare for the day when we will run out of petroleum. Since then, oil and natural gas have been discovered in the most unlikely places in all parts of the world and deep under the ocean bottom. We are still energy-secure albeit heavily dependent on imports from unstable sources. Twice in the 1970's our vulnerability was brought home to us in ways that plagued us with distress and threatened our economy. Weighty words were uttered that it was high time for our nation to develop a policy to assure adequate energy for the future, and some tentative steps were taken. We had delayed too long, and it took two crises to rouse us from our lethargy. But the dislocations were short-lived, and the same torpor set in again.

It is a human weakness to postpone unpleasant choices that include such economic insults as import quotas, tariffs, higher fuel taxes, and most of all, self-denial in a country of plenty. It is also human foible to find scapegoats when unwelcome choices confront us. In place of devising an energy policy, we pinned the tail on the oil companies that daily risk billions in a resourceful search for hydrocarbons in secure venues and rightfully profit from their endeavors. But there is no longer time for waffling or procrastination, now that we have a reprieve from energy disaster. A choice must be made.

At times, we evade choices by seconding them to others whom we pay to make them for us. How else could we have become the most litigious society on earth? It may take fortitude to eschew an attractive proposition because, on close examination, it carries unacceptable risks. It may be inconvenient to investigate the efficacy of a product or service and the guarantees offered with it. It may be undiplomatic to lock horns over the terms of agreements we seek to shape to our advantage. And why should we? We can abdicate such decisions to the legal profession and the judiciary with the result that we have become an adversarial society. Our dealings with government and with each other have become mired in a morass of regulation and recrimination from which we are hard put to extricate ourselves. Free men and women though we think we are, the truth is that we have chained ourselves to the slippery pole of mistrust that inhibits our freedom to act. There is a fatal weakness in this. It prevents us from taking the bold steps, as individuals and as a nation, demanded by the continual challenges from within and without to our ability to govern ourselves.

Self-determination gives way to enslavement when we shun the responsibility for making choices that affect us, even in petty ways.

Sometimes our reluctance to make choices is prompted by fear. Nothing else could account for the tentative steps we take under duress to accord civil equality to those who, unaccountably, fail to measure up to preconceived notions about human worth. It smacks suspiciously of xenophobia. Whatever brought new strangers to our shores—we were all strangers once—cannot, by any logic, play a role in how they are accepted by the establishment. Whether as slaves, fugitives from tyranny, or entrepreneurs seeking greater opportunity, they all arrived with hopes. Some adapted more readily, others with some difficulty. Slaves had to wait two centuries before they were freed at all, and their descendants even longer before they attained a small measure of civil stature.

Ironically, our problem is not with xenophobia at all. We exhibit no fear of a Belgian banker who settles here; we reserve it for the third-world immigrant, and skin color has little to do with it. Our real dread is of the growth of an underclass beyond our control. There are two ways to deal with this: one is to offer economic opportunities that preclude an underclass and, with it, the threat of violent behavior. The other is to accept a two-tier social structure and the high cost of containing the anti-social lifestyles to which an underclass is forced to resort. We have yet to make that choice and, instead, attribute our fears to racial and ethnic differences.

Every responsible person would agree that it is prudent to live within one's means. Few would dispute that this country's federal budget deficit has been, at best, undesirable and uneconomic. To reduce it and eventually restore the nation's finances to an even keel involves choices nobody seems willing to make. The only mandatory budget item that cannot be pared is the interest on our huge national debt. Virtually everything else can. It can, that is, if each constituency were to renounce all or some of what it seeks from the government—from a powerful defense establishment to the most trivial pork-barrel entitlement. Each constituency believes in the justifiability of its special interest and expends enormous energy to prove it. Lost in this Babel is the rationale for making budgets in the first place, which is to separate the feasible from the illusory, the necessity from the luxury. Wealthy as our country may be, there are limits to its fiscal resources that can be raised only when our productivity generates sufficient revenues as it has in the current boom. Even then, we must draw a delicate balance of an adequate living standard, on the one hand, and to provide for national growth on the other.

Admittedly, this is a difficult balance to achieve and totally impossible when no one will budge in deference to higher priorities. It is a fiscal game of chicken in which nobody grants the right of way to another until faced with disaster. Assessing the true value of one's priorities is a subtle art that demands choices one is inclined to make only when everyone else is doing likewise. What is clearly needed now is a national resolve to choose fairly among the programs deemed universally indispensable and those that satisfy only a marginal few. Are we prepared to make such choices?

Choices must be made with conviction. What happens when resolve fails to match bravado is demonstrated by two events. In Vietnam, we ran away from responsibility for choices. Some believed ours to be the only nation with the military strength to salvage what the French could not in Southeast Asia. Others advocated intervention to forestall the tumble of Asian dominoes to Communist aggression. Arrayed against them were evolutionists who saw the conflict as the inevitable disintegration of one of the last colonial empires. The arguments matter little. It does matter that a clear choice was never made about U.S. involvement in Vietnam. It never is when hostilities begin with deployment of military advisors, followed by small armed contingents to protect the advisors, followed by full-scale military support for those already committed to the battle scene. Contrast this with the clear choice, supported by all Americans, to fight after the Pearl Harbor attack, or even the U.S. entry into World War I, ostensibly triggered by the sinking of the Lusitania. In both cases, Americans responded with a clear-cut decision to engage in war.

No wonder many people believe the Vietnam War could not have been won, given our national ambivalence rather than hostile terrain. Individual heroism was certainly not lacking. There is a valid school of thought which holds that, had America's survival been on the line, a more determined strategy could have brought military victory even in those jungles.

Closer to home, millions of Americans read George Bush's lips and elected him to make good on his promise of no new taxes. But no sooner had he sworn the oath of office than he was labeled a disappointment for acceding to higher taxes as an antidote to deficits. Discounting the motives of those bent on embarrassing the new President, what are we to make of such two-headedness? If, as a people, we truly believed that new and higher imposts were the answer, we had ample opportunity to elect an outspoken exponent of higher taxes. What kind of choice was this?

And what kind of choice is it to elect administrations that promise to reduce the size of the bureaucracy. A presidential candidate can do himself no greater good, it seems, than to promise to get government off people's backs. It is a guaranteed applause line. Of course, that should mean the abolition of countless regulatory procedures governing the private sector, with all their reporting and compliance requirements. It should be axiomatic that he who foots the bill has an implied right to monitor how the money is spent and to promulgate rules for its custodianship—and the government does just that. Government is on our backs because we cheerfully accept its generosity. A government that does not intrude on private life cannot deliver social services, guarantee home and student loans, or subsidize all sorts of peripheral ventures of the private sector. The size and scope of government, a 200-million population notwithstanding, may have gotten out of hand. One need only recall the cadre that managed the country's business in George Washington's administration, though, admittedly, we cannot return to square one. But it takes a brave choice to redefine the role of government. Instead, we excoriate the very officials we just helped to elect.

This explains why most office-holders follow the middle road even when they campaigned on a platform of radical change. Somehow, they discover the instinct that tells them the electorate would be dismayed to find its strong opinions embodied in drastic action by their elected officials. They quickly learn to cater to the people's timidity by responding with mediocrity. Whatever its origin, our shirking of choices bespeaks a weakness that may some day cost us dearly as a nation. Beyond platitudes, it becomes increasingly difficult to define what this country stands for. As a result, we send mixed signals abroad and, at home, confuse those who must guide our national destiny.

We can and must do better than that. We must regain our ability, as a people, to make difficult choices and stand by them.

Taking Risks I

Nowhere is a society's strength better expressed than in its willingness and ability to take risks. We are not concerned here with such risk-taking as arises from skydiving or taking a flier in the stock market, though these may help illustrate a cardinal point. Essentially, a risk is a trade-off—a willingness to lose one asset in the pursuit of another. Skydivers, for instance, receive a momentous thrill—a thrill that I, for one, cannot appreciate—from the free fall they execute before their parachutes open. In exchange for those spine-tingling moments they seem prepared to lose their lives in the event their maneuvers go awry or their chutes fail to open. To my mind, the ratio between risk and reward suggests some very long odds, but to the devotee, convinced of his skill and reliant on some intensive training, it is a fair proposition. The stock-market speculator deals with somewhat less daunting dangers. He sees financial success and a lifetime of ease at the end of a preferably short rainbow, knowing full well that a miscalculation or adversity in the market could leave him considerably poorer than when he began.

Irrelevant as these examples may seem, they illustrate a critical facet of the choices life forces upon us if it is to be lived with character. Making a choice is a process of ordering one's priorities. It is also the skill of evaluating the negative consequences of losing either of the assets at risk—the one we are willing to gamble away and the one we seek to gain. In the business world they refer to these as the upside and downside risks. And the way the upside and downside are assessed determines that blend of wisdom and courage from which we extrapolate the nature of our national character.

As a devout coward, I cannot conceive of a single thrill for which I am prepared to have my bones broken. As a timid investor, I have never lusted after riches whose attainment might place my financial security in jeopardy. Still, like any sensible person, I am aware that virtually any pursuit may entail some risk. A perfectly harmless game of cards can become so engrossing that one may forget to take the stew off the stove and burn the dinner or even set the kitchen on fire. Here, however, the risk is minuscule and the reward reasonable.

In moments of crisis, the ratio tends to shift. With a seriously ill loved one in the car, a normally cautious driver is apt to speed and run through stop lights en route to the hospital—a ride that might well give him nightmares in retrospect. Rationally or not, he has suddenly rearranged his priorities to favor his patient over the integrity of his automobile or even his own safety. This explains such tales of heroism as Samaritans diving into freezing water to save a drowning swimmer or running into a blazing house to rescue a trapped victim. More subtle shifts of priorities occur when someone forgoes assured profits to expand a business or threatens to quit his job if a raise is not forthcoming. In wartime, personal priorities disappear almost completely. Commanded by superior officers to face death, the soldier no longer considers his risk and makes the command his objective. Such choices as he has left in the circumstances stem partly from his natural reflexes in making the riskier move lest the safer one proves ultimately even more destructive. Indeed, it is this aberration in risk assessment learned in war during formative years that leads more unfortunate veterans into self-destructive and tragic careers when they return to civilian life.

It seems likely, in fact, that our risk-taking proclivities are established at a point far earlier than the time they express themselves in our lifestyles. I leave it to psychiatrists to explain, if they can, why gamblers gamble and others take unconscionable chances. Far more significant is the allocation of priorities as they bear on our national character and visceral strength. Life becomes unmanageable when risks must be weighed every step along the way. Where the gambler throws caution to the winds, it is just as destructive to consider every potential pitfall before venturing out on one's accustomed rounds. There are potential hazards in every workaday activity, in the home and outside. Common-sense precautions are commendable but when they fail to suffice an emotional imbalance results and we cease to function as normal human beings. Recluses, whose neighbors have not seen them in years, may be diagnosed as suffering from a number of possible mental ailments, but, in the last analysis, these loners have concluded that the risks of venturing into the everyday world are too great. Just as important, they have lost sight of the rewards that come from functioning in conventional ways. They have clearly ceased to be productive members of society and whatever talents they possess are lost to the community at large. Because of their aversion to risk, they become easy prey for evildoers; their households, not to mention their lives, are in disarray.

The national psyche is not much different. Its strength is in direct proportion to its ability to select rationally between the peacetime activities for which risk must be assessed and those to which every effort must be bent without constant attention to the possibility of grief.

Our manic concern with the environment provides a good case in point. Much of what threatens the environment today is a result of activities associated with normal national life; at least, life as it is and must be lived at the turn of the new century.

Concern with environment is hardly new. It can be interpreted to date to ancient religious proscriptions concerning cleanliness. In modern times, there are few communities that do not have ordinances against spitting on the sidewalk or improper disposal of garbage. By and large, however, purity of air and water were concerns for which our forefathers had little time and patience, attentive as they were to the more basic tasks of building a thriving nation. If objections arose to new rights of way of railroads as they spread westward, they were predicated on usurpation of farming lands, not on smoke the old locomotives might belch. The economic value of railroads far outweighed environmental fears. To be sure, pioneers learned early to keep their cesspools and privies far from their wells for drinking water. It was a matter of common sense to them, not a preoccupation. Today, the demands of modern society are more ambitious. We gobble up electric power which, when not available from hydro-electric sources, must be generated with giant oil- or coal-fired furnaces. We insist on a high degree of mobility dependent primarily on fossil fuels that perforce emit fumes. Industry is largely fueled by oil and natural gas and, since we have learned the pitfalls of dependence on foreign oil sources, we seem determined to become as self-sufficient as possible. This means drilling for oil wherever there is a likelihood of finding it, and refining it and transporting it across public roads and pristine waters. Petrochemicals are essential to virtually every convenience of modern life and these, too, must be manufactured somewhere. And while we are gradually phasing out coal as a primary fuel, we are learning how to convert it to alternative fuels and are busily mining it from strip mines in previously unspoiled regions.

Under the obsolescing ethic of accepting necessary trade-offs to make our nation strong and great, the hazards were not only deemed acceptable; they were ignored much like a stable hand ignores horse droppings in pursuit of his calling. Was any harm done? Of course, it was. Coal miners suffered and died from lung disease, but through it all they regarded theirs as an honorable, though perhaps lowly and dangerous profession. If injustice was done them, it was their exploitation through shamefully inadequate wages and disregard for their hardships. Today, hazardous-duty pay incentives are the norm and should have been right along. Under the old ethic, pioneers crossed the plains in wagon trains without protection against the weather and marauding

Indians, and without any guarantee that, at the end of the line, life would be livable. Safety devices were unheard of in the early days of American industry. Instead, neighbors banded together to help distressed families when a fellow worker came to grief.

Along with our progress in technology itself, we have made comparable strides in harnessing the dangers it thrust upon us. There are safer ways to mine natural resources and produce the myriad goods on which modern society depends. We know more about protecting ourselves in ways that should not seriously interfere with the pursuit of our goals. We are more adept in avoiding unnecessary risks. But we have also become too preoccupied with risks that, in a more courageous climate, would be acceptable and dealt with as coming with the territory. We now have a government agency that tells us how to use a ladder safely; and woe to the offender who fails to pay proper attention to its dicta. Ladders in one form or another have been used throughout recorded history. Their use was regarded as a necessary risk and one generation passed along to the next the knack of using them safely. The deliberate use of a defective ladder would incur public wrath; society devised its own safety incentives.

Nothing demonstrates this more emphatically than our attitude toward nuclear energy. During the depths of the oil shortages of the 1970's, it seemed clear that nuclear power was indispensable to our energy security. With present technology, it would not drive automobiles or fly airplanes, our largest consumers of petroleum, but it could take the pressure off oil demand by doing virtually everything else—heat and cool homes and keep the wheels of industry turning. France and other western European countries had already established nuclear power as a pivotal source of energy. And so, presumably, had the Soviet Union. But now that the pressure is off, timidity of unprecedented proportions has taken over.

One must wonder what might have been had the circumstances attending the birth of atomic energy been less violent; if, instead of being unveiled to the world in the searing infernos of Hiroshima and Nagasaki, nuclear power had first been demonstrated as a peaceful laboratory device with great potential as a new alternative energy source. Surely, the image of the mushroom cloud would not now distort what should be sober consideration of the benefits to be derived from harnessing the atom as a useful genie. Just as surely, scientists would have been aware of the hazards to public safety that must be overcome by painstaking design and operation of nuclear power plants. And probably there would be those who would caution against their use because an accident could be more destructive than a mishap at a conventional powerhouse. But the risks would be more clearly defined and the ratio to reward assessed with an even hand.

To be sure, a nuclear miscalculation cannot be dismissed casually. The mishaps at Three Mile Island and Chernobyl illustrate the extremes. The former, though momentarily frightening and very costly in the long run, did not result in a meltdown, caused no destruction of public property and no discernable personal injury. At Chernobyl there was an incipient meltdown, contamination did spread beyond Soviet borders, and there were loss of life and injury. Both instances provided examples of what can happen when the downside risk prevails, but in the resulting tumult the upside tends to be ignored. The fact is that Three Mile Island and other plants like it provide electricity to large areas economically, and consumers are not about to alter their lifestyles by curtailing their use of power or by paying more for it. In the case of Chernobyl, it must be presumed that the Soviets were in dire need of an efficient power source in that area and determined a nuclear plant to be the most effective way to provide it; so much so, perhaps, that construction of the plant could not await newer and safer technology or operational safeguards. Risks may have been taken but, then, if the downside were never to occur, there would be no risks to take.

The mass hysteria that impeded completion of the Seabrook nuclear plant in New Hampshire and literally scuttled the completed Shoreham facility in Long Island bespeaks a frightening inability by people to confront risks. Few would argue that both areas would not benefit from these plants. It may be true that cost overruns in their construction compromised their economic efficiency and, in the final analysis, rendered them unattractive as energy alternatives. But, to some degree, even their exorbitant costs were occasioned by the refusal of their beneficiaries to take risks plainly associated with life in the twentieth and twenty-first centuries. Even as the public clamor for safe evacuation of Long Island in case of a mishap at Shoreham began to die down—Long Island being a natural cul-de-sac—new outcries began to arise because of the alternative risk. With Shoreham out of play, plans were being made to import electricity through high-capacity power lines into Long Island via high-tension conduits. And a new outcry began to arise—this time against the radiation from the conduits as it might affect health along the proposed routes.

With urban populations growing and demanding ever greater supplies of electric power, we see an abject denial of risk. Were this a perfect world, ways of providing this power without any drawbacks might be devised. But this is a clear-cut case of refusal to assess the value of the objective—adequate power—against the value of the matter at risk—absolute safety. The Europeans understood this choice quite well, and they opted for the progress that was indispensable to them. Fully 70% of the electric power generated in France is nuclear. In Germany it is 22% . Spain has 33%. But the United States has less than 10%. Lest we underestimate the Europeans, let us be certain that they, too, are aware of the potential risks, but they made a clear choice. If the ability to take risks is any indication of national determination, the United States has something to worry about.

Much has been written about the prospect of lesser nations overtaking us as economic powers and, in the very distant future, as military powers as well. While this is not a present danger, even in the face of Japan's and Germany's industrial prowess, we cannot dismiss a fact of life: less developed countries are doing now what the United States did in a former century. They are accepting risks that are no longer acceptable to us. Wherever possible, they take sensible precautions, many of them learned from us, but they refuse to let risks stand in the way of progress. It is interesting to note that Germany, after more than fifty years of phenomenal postwar industrial progress, may also follow us into this trap under the misguidance of the Greenpeace movement which demands, like our environmentalists, that all risks be eliminated before a spade can be turned. Japan is seeing the development of a similar trend, spurred to some extent by that nation's confinement to a chain of small islands.

One frightening sign of our submission to risk avoidance is the glee with which American manufacturers, to the applause of their customers, turn to so-called cheap labor in less developed nations. This is a delusion. It is not cheap labor that beckons American business as much as it is uninhibited labor. Deprived people in backward countries nurture an aggressive work ethic in which caution is often thrown to the winds as they claw their way up the economic ladder. This may reflect itself in the labor costs that attract our business. The disaster at Bhopal brought this to our national consciousness. The laxity that made the Bhopal accident possible would never have passed muster in any of our fifty states. But then this is why Bhopal was a seemingly logical place to manufacture insecticides, largely for consumption in the United States. When all is said and done, the years of activity at the plant brought Bhopal prosperity and social strength, albeit measured by the modest terms of a generally impoverished society. Expressed another way, the people of Bhopal, in their zeal to upgrade the quality of their lives, ignored or even accepted a large risk for a reward that seemed justifiable to them.

If we have lost the courage to take social risks, our performance in dealing with personal risk has become even more dismal. While good health is to be cherished and long life to be applauded, they have become baals at whose altars we sacrifice much of what gives us satisfaction and pleasure; and the question arises whether long, healthy life is an end in itself. A wise friend ventured that preoccupation with health and longevity is an affectation of the well-heeled; for them, life is too much fun to be cut short. This may be true. Table conversation about the dangers of eating steak is more likely to be heard in the homes of the wealthy. Those deprived of such luxuries are accustomed to living a day-to-day existence that, when occasionally larded with the presumed no-nos of food and drink, becomes just a little brighter. For the most unfortunate among us long life is probably a curse.

Part of the blame may well rest with the medical technologies we glorify. I have lived long enough to remember when the infirmities of advanced age were regarded as just that and were commonly accepted as precursors of inexorable death. And in a time before science overtook faith as our chief source of comfort, even the tragic illness and death of a young person could be embraced as the workings and wisdom of a higher authority. This is no longer so. Medical science now enables us to scrutinize the minutest parts of our anatomies and, based on the findings, steer a circuitous route to our ultimate demise—so tortuous, in fact, that we have taken to squabbling over the ethics of keeping a cadaver among the living by use of sophisticated machinery.

Life is one continuous risk, and its grand mystery is that we never know when or how we will lose it. To focus all our energies—or to divert ourselves from the pursuit of worthier objectives and pleasures—merely to stave off the time of death or physical disintegration is to gainsay the risk we assumed in the birth canal. Our resolve to live life to the fullest has become so enfeebled that we fall prey to every admonition of impending doom if we persist in following our instincts. We are becoming a nation of wimps.

Thirty years ago, the Surgeon General warned that cigarette smoking could be injurious to our health, and he used the most spurious of statistics. We timidly accepted the proposition that 85% of patients who died from lung cancer were smokers, never reflecting on its true meaning. It was the same as saying that 85% of those who died in airplane crashes were flying in planes. True enough; but it is a far cry from saying that 85% of people aboard planes die in crashes. Nor do 85% of all smokers succumb to lung cancer. And not a word about lung cancer among nonsmokers. But in our timidity, we have accepted the new gospel which has since been expanded to include potential health damage from so-called secondary smoke inhaled by those in the company of smokers. Even if the Surgeon General were persuasive, what guarantee will he give the nonsmoker that a truck will not run amok and snuff him out like a cigarette butt?

Nobody would suggest that smoking is a particularly health-giving habit or that everyone should relish the aroma of tobacco. But the absurdity of our surrender to fear can be measured by the way nonsmokers, especially former smokers, now recoil at even the faintest trace of tobacco aroma. If there is a threat in tobacco products, it stems from the smoke that emanates directly from the flame burning in the cigarette, cigar or pipe. Once that flame is out, the remaining aroma is no more threatening than the aroma of a pungent stew on the stove. Of course, not everybody likes the smell of stew, either.

What this panic completely ignores is the psychological lift smokers derive from their use of tobacco. Not a drug-like high, perhaps, but an ability to function a little more smoothly, to behave a little more sociably—in short, to feel a little better. Nonsmokers and those who kicked the habit may argue that they function just as well without smoking. For some this may be true and for others it may be self-delusion. More important, however, those who persist in smoking are taking the sensible risk that there are other objectives to be attained in life and that their attainment becomes more facile, or seemingly so, with a cigarette, cigar or pipe at hand. They simply refuse to succumb to the threats of doomsayers in the pursuit either of important goals or even of the simple pleasure of relaxing with a smoke.

What can be said of tobacco seems true also of alcohol. The risks differ somewhat. Where a smoke can make someone more efficient at his desk, alcohol usually has the opposite effect. And no one has ever been faulted in an accident for having smoked before he drove. Historically, alcoholic beverages have been a mainstay of conviviality. Tastes have varied through history. Once it was the grape that bespoke good fellowship—and even religious worship—and at other times preferences have run to the hardier brews distilled from grain, potatoes or rice. The ingredients of the drink matter little, for they all produce a euphoric effect; eased tensions and heightened humor. Taken to excess, they can also foster hostility, irresponsibility and lack of self-control. But excessive drinking, like any excessive indulgence, skews the risk-to-reward ratio, and it is to the credit of a person to assess such risks in their proper perspective. As for those physiologically prone to alcohol addiction, they are well advised to abstain in the same way people with weak hearts should eschew mountain climbing.

Some people equate virtue with abstinence from both drinking and smoking. This is a total misconception of virtue. Avoiding risks at all costs is anything but a virtue. Rather, it is a sign of timidity that leads to reliance on a fool's faith—that by avoiding small pleasures we can be spared the rigors of living and dying. Down that road lies a defeatism which, in time, could contaminate our entire national psyche. The risks of living and dying cannot be avoided. Hence we should use them daily as bargaining chips in our pursuit of whatever we perceive as our individual and collective missions.

Why is life so to be treasured that we are willing to forgo living just to preserve it? This is the question we might ask that cautious soul who whets his appetite with a bracing glass of club soda; who looks lovingly at a piece of fish surrounded by lightly poached veggies; in whose diet salt plays absolutely no role; who cannot remember the last time he had bacon and eggs for breakfast and instead selects warily among cereals ostensibly concocted to protect the arteries; for whom a piece of fruit has become the only permissible dessert; who, worst of all, believes he has thus vouchsafed for himself something approaching immortality. Fear of food has taken on such ludicrous proportions that a wholesome barbecue is to be shunned because of the potential carcinogenicity of charcoal; that fruit and vegetables must be organically grown and untainted by preservatives; that cheese, when eaten at all, must be free of the milk fats that make it appealing in the first place; that, indeed, the entire process of feeding ourselves becomes an exercise in paranoia and self-denial.

In these misconceptions we are abetted by a medical establishment that has either lost its perspective or adopted an ill-intentioned agenda of its own. Knowing better than anyone that life is finite, it plies us with warnings and restrictions which create the illusion that immortality is almost attainable. The image of the physician as one to whom we turn to alleviate pain has given way to that of an oracle whose wisdom and high-priced ministrations can prevent it. To some degree the modern doctor can do that, and it is only proper that he should try. But the attempt can lead to excesses and it probably has.

It was only in recent decades that serum cholesterol has been identified as the culprit that, in time, can clog arteries and cause heart disease. Those at high risk understandably took the warnings to heart. Those with no discernible need to worry seized on them as a panacea. And as they dutifully perform and abstain in accordance with medical dicta, the standards to which they are urged to adhere, like shifting sands, are repeatedly raised in order to intimidate them into even more rigorous performance and abstinence. Weights and cholesterol counts once pronounced safe have since been declared borderline hazardous and new, lower targets have been set by the medical experts. And those who dared rest easy with seemingly acceptable cholesterol levels are now cautioned to distinguish between high-and low-density cholesterol and to look over their shoulders for the menace of triglycerides.

There is no limit to caution. No blemish must go unscanned, we are warned, and no change of mood escape therapy. As if it mattered, we are urged to submit to all sorts of diagnostic procedures, if only to give a name to the dysfunction that ultimately does us in.

In the end, all life comes to the same finality. It is of little importance that what we once accepted as old-age infirmity can now be diagnosed precisely. The body, like any organism, loses it resistance to the ravages of life, no matter how cautiously lived. Its ability to shrug off infections, reinvigorate failing organs, mend broken bones and resist the proliferation of malignant cells diminishes as we grow older. In some people the process takes longer and less time in others. But somewhere along the line we succumb to the ultimate physical breakdown, and all we have refused to risk comes to naught. This was brought home to me poignantly by a journalism professor during a class in writing obituaries. Never, he warned, report that the subject died suddenly. Everybody dies suddenly; one second we are alive and the next second we are dead.

Therein lies the essence of risk-taking. One never knows when the object at risk will have to be sacrificed. Therefore, every moment spent, every heroic effort bent to preserve it is a moment we should use productively—as individuals and as a nation. To succeed in the quests we set as tasks before us, we must keep our eye on the objective to be gained and not on the asset to be lost lest we risk losing both. It is an inescapable trade-off.

Once we, as a nation, have lost touch with this reality, our vitality is sorely threatened. It will give us little solace then to predict that those who might surpass us in various fields of endeavor might also drink and smoke themselves to death. While American tourists look on appalled, our competitors abroad operate in smoke-filled places. They relax over life-threatening meals framed by aperitifs, wine, beer, and cognac. And they plow ahead in their ambitious pursuits considering only those risks as may thwart success, not the petty fear of wearing their bodies out in the process. They are like bees in a hive, humming furiously away at making honey before the clock runs out on their short life span. How can we overcome competition like that?

The Free Lunch

Every year the U.S. government spends billions to serve what can best be described as a free lunch. For the edification of those born after the era of these repasts, free lunch was the term for the buffet meals offered without charge by drinking establishments of an earlier time. For a nickel one could buy a glass of beer at the bar and then turn to the opposite wall where a buffet rich with sliced meats, bread and trimmings awaited. No proprietor would be so gauche as to interfere with hungry freeloaders, but ethics demanded the purchase of at least one beer.

Today, the saying goes, there is no more free lunch. But the government serves it up in the guise of entitlement programs that make free snacks pale by comparison. As with the nickel beer, the government exacts a seemingly small price in the form of taxes—small when one compares a typical taxpayer's contribution with the overall largess available in return. Entitlement programs now constitute the third largest slice of the federal budget, right behind mandated costs, such as interest on government bonds, payment of prior purchase commitments, and outlays for national defense.

To understand these so-called entitlements, we must go back to the 1930's, when the American economy literally fell apart and, some say, a popular revolt could be averted only by Draconian measures to help those who simply could not help themselves in the circumstances. Millions of Americans had no jobs and no prospects of finding employment as potential employers were up against it also. Many were forced to turn to soup kitchens in lieu of the three square meals most of us now take for granted. And while the term homeless did not have the cachet it has now, families were threatened with eviction for nonpayment of rent. If, indeed, they were spared, it was largely because landlords had no prospects of replacing them and wisely figured that something would give and, with someone in the premises, they could cut their losses when recovery ultimately came.

Those fortunate enough to own their homes were unable to meet their mortgage payments and faced foreclosure, as did countless farmers whose debts mounted with little hope of selling their crops and preserving their ownership. Some thought themselves wise to have salted away some savings in banks but woke up to the reality that their banks were insolvent and their nest eggs lost or at least in jeopardy.

It was an intolerable situation; one that, in less stable nations, would have spawned revolution. Only two factors prevented an American uprising. One was the popular recognition that there was really nobody against whom to rise up; virtually everybody was in the same boat except the extremely wealthy who, it was generally conceded, were not at fault since the calamity did not result from plutocratic oppression. Nor was there an identifiable proletariat in the United States. Even in abject poverty, Americans continued to think of themselves as members of the middle class.

To illustrate this, the story is told of a meeting at which Eric Johnston, the American movie czar, was asked by Josef Stalin: "When will the Americans have their proletarian revolution?" To which Johnston replied: "How can there be a proletarian revolution in America when we have no proletariat?"

The second deterrent to a potential revolt was the sweeping intervention by the Roosevelt Administration to stem the public bleeding almost immediately after taking office. To debate here whether some of the actions taken had been conceived, at least in principle, by the outgoing government of Herbert Hoover is to cloud the issue. To be charitable about it, we must concede that no administration could safely have tolerated the situation any longer, and it becomes a matter of conjecture what Hoover might have done had he remained in office after 1933.

Instead, the issue focuses on the concept that government can step in on a crisis and perform economic surgery when the private sector is hemorrhaging. Out of this intervention came some notable innovations which, while they fell far short of setting things right, at least stabilized the mechanisms that make a free economy tick. The bank holiday defused the run on the institutions that were unable to pay their depositors on demand. The disentanglement of banks from the securities brokerage business probably helped save both businesses from collapse. And there followed the creation of numerous government agencies, such as the Federal Reserve System and the Securities and Exchange Commission, to monitor various aspects of economic life and to manage phases of the economy, when necessary, in order to prevent abuse from being heaped upon disaster in a time of crisis.

But the most pervasive trend of that period was the appearance of government agencies charged with priming the pump, in the parlance of the day, that is to say to assume the role of entrepreneur when private enterprise seemed hopelessly sagging.

To assist the homeless and those with aspirations for homes of their own, the government created the Federal Housing Administration for the purpose of insuring home mortgages against foreclosure. This served to give banks the courage to lend money to home buyers who could offer only small down payments and even smaller secure income with which to pay interest and principal. Thus, the banks rested assured that any home owner's default would be met by the F.H.A.

For those frustrated in their search for employment, Washington established the Public Works Administration and the Work Progress Administration, both of which undertook construction projects of facilities for public use, thereby creating employment that was lacking in the private sector. For the young—those whose credentials would not qualify them for jobs in a tight market—there was the Civilian

Conservation Corps that provided gainful activities combined with on-the-job training in the nation's natural-resource areas.

To revive public confidence in the banking system, the New Deal Administration established the Federal Deposit Insurance Corporation, funded and empowered to replace deposited funds, up to $10,000 per depositor in those days, in the event a failing bank lacked liquid assets. The plight of the elderly, many of whom had lost or were forced to use up their life's savings, was addressed with the formation of the Social Security Administration, conceived as a sort of public annuity. Social Security's praiseworthy record of paying subsistence from day one to retirees even before contributions could match the payout was a feat of financial planning. There was also the Rural Electrification Administration which, along with an intricate system of farm subsides, infused new strength into America's agricultural industry. Many others followed.

There is some disagreement over whether this array of interventionist activity by the government would, by itself, have restored America to complete economic health within a known time frame, but the question is academic. Along came World War II and, even before U.S. entry into the fighting, industrial activity began to soar in an effort to supply our allies and to arm ourselves for the day of inevitable American involvement in the conflict. Oversupply gave way to demand for scarce goods needed for the defense effort. Employment rose smartly, especially as manpower was drained away by military conscription. Both wages and prices increased as the demand for both people and goods increased. The Great Depression was over.

As a concomitant, however, there was a perceived need for more government intervention of another sort. To prevent price-gouging in a suddenly bloating economy, there was the Office of Price Administration. To channel labor and materials into the most productive uses there were the War Manpower Administration and the War Production Board. And a bevy of lesser agencies coped with the unprecedented contingencies of an unprecedented war.

Throughout this entire period, the nation's tax structure changed and magnified. People previously exempt from income taxes found themselves suddenly included in the taxpayers' ranks. Pay-as-you-go taxing, devised by Beardsley Ruml, a department store executive, became the norm and survives today as tax withholding not only by employers but by interest- and dividend-paying institutions. The shock of coughing up a year's taxes by March 15 was too much for an entire segment of the public unaccustomed to paying taxes at all. Whether by design or force of circumstances, this evolution in taxation also suggested a possibly hidden plan to redistribute wealth in the United States. Ostensibly, higher revenue income was needed by the government merely to finance many newfound functions it performed during the Depression and the ensuing war effort. And while it subjected lower-income citizens to income taxes for the first time, its greatest impact was on big business and the upper strata of personal wealth. There is an irony in this. Logic would lead us to believe that if, indeed, there was some intended or accidental redistribution of wealth, we should be seeing a greater degree of comity between upper and lower income groups. Exactly the opposite seems to have occurred. There is probably greater class consciousness today than there was before the Depression, fueled in part by the more recently developed sense of racial and ethnic identity in which minorities see themselves as the underclass.

Ironically, where there was no American proletariat in the past, a self-proclaimed one now seems to exist, or more to the point, wants to exist. There is no denying that we have pockets of extreme poverty and ghettos of seeming hopelessness. But they are the creation not of the absence of prosperity, but rather the yearning for the free lunch.

People have become accustomed to relying on government for whatever is difficult to come by through their own efforts. This is not to denigrate either the disadvantaged who genuinely need help or the individual mechanisms the government contrived to meet specialized needs. Rather it is to identify a state of mind that invites the government into an increasing variety of vacuums that people themselves are reluctant to fill. This indolence is not the making of the poor, but rather of those who should be well able to muster the necessary ingenuity and resourcefulness to fend for themselves.

Thus we delude ourselves that home ownership, in whatever form, is something to be attained without a struggle; that savings will yield interest whenever they are taken to a building with glass doors and a maze of ropes leading to a teller's cage; that a cart full of plastic-wrapped groceries will provide wholesome nourishment without further scrutiny; that medical bills will be manageable and the doctor's prescription be effective; that trains and planes will arrive on schedule; that automobiles will be safe to drive without any driver involvement; even that a chance to make big money will not be fraught with risk.

If this seems like a tall order, the government seems willing to serve it up. To understand, one must consider what constitutes government. It consists of elected officials with an overpowering urge to hold on to their jobs and always at the mercy of the electorate. There is no surer road to defeat at the polls than to advocate the abolition of Social Security or, nowadays, to ignore the environment. Indulgence of the public in its delusions constitutes job security for elected officials.

This is as it should be as long as nobody has devised a better system of government—and predictably nobody will. It is inherently a good system—the best in the world. But it is a system of consensus in a society that is, by nature, pluralistic. In other words, you have to please all of the people all of the time. And any parent will tell you that indulging a child all of the time will produce a brat.

And so, like an overindulged child acting up when it fails to get its way, people take to the streets with placards whenever the government's gifts fall short of expectations. The right to make our voices heard is one of the precious freedoms guaranteed under the First Amendment. Thus it is not the form of protest that is fearsome, but the causes for which so many demonstrations are organized. Most frequently, they focus on what the demonstrators perceive as a lapse in the government's attention to their particular needs and wants. Sometimes they are monetary, and often they concern policies that cause discontent among certain interest groups. However, they all seem predicated on the assumption that, if no one else will do the job, the government ultimately will.

Naturally, each interest group can make a plausible case for its protest. If Medicare reimbursements appear inadequate to the recipients, theirs seems like a just reason to raise their voices for more comprehensive health care programs. If reduced fiscal support of child care programs threatens supervision of their youngsters, working parents feel entitled to protest. When the products of an overdeveloped civilization pollute water or air, environmentalists take to their podiums to condemn the government for not policing sufficiently the technologies that give us countless products and conveniences without which life has become unthinkable. When, in the exigencies of trying to make ends meet in Washington and the state capitals, funds for cultural or educational ventures are pared, the cry of foul is heard from those quarters. It is merely a question of whose ox is being gored, with each segment of society claiming its due.

Collectively, however, it becomes a clamor for more, more and more. For decades the din competed in volume with demands that the federal budget be brought into balance. Now that it has—and the booming economy has blessed us with a surplus for the years ahead—we find ourselves embroiled in controversy over how this new-found fiscal cushion is to be spent.

In trying to achieve budget balance before prosperity came to our aid, the Gramm-Rudman-Hollings Act attempted to provide the mechanical guidelines for achieving balance over time. But it would have been effective only on condition that it be adhered to without compromise, since the same accounting methods could also be perverted to camouflage imbalance. Zero-base budgeting is another helpmate. It offers the government—and supposedly the public—an opportunity to examine each spending program afresh to determine each year whether its raison d'être continues to be valid. And if zero-base budgeting were to be instituted, my guess is that the clamor for each of the entitlements would be raised annually as each benefit program comes up for scrutiny. There simply is no way of cramming ten pounds of sausage into a five-pound casing.

To some extent, profligacy could be reduced by giving the President the much needed line-item veto, a tool already available to the governors of 43 states. It would enable a President to strike from an appropriations bill those particular items he considers excessive without the need to veto an entire bill that contains desirable or unavoidable expenditures. The line-item veto is no cure-all, but it might help trim the fat from government's servings and leave the meat intact.

Part of the problem is the proclivity of government to expand basic programs to provide new variations that might benefit another group of citizens. Housing programs offer a good example, but just one of many.

When the government established the Federal Housing Administration, its basic function was to assure mortgage lenders that, in case of default by the homeowner, the government would make up the loss. For this insurance, the FHA charged a premium of one-quarter of one percent that, as far as the homeowner was concerned, became part of the interest rate, but which the banks remitted to the government to hold in reserve against potential defaults.

Ingenious as this idea may have been, and regardless of the millions whom it helped attain home ownership, it propelled the government further into the paternalism that underlies many of the problems we face today. Perhaps it seemed only fair that assistance should also be provided for those who chose to remain tenants. This could be accomplished by making it more affordable for developers to build apartment units by offering them a similar package of low equity investments—equivalent to small down payments—and insuring their mortgages against default. And so FHA-insured apartment buildings sprouted up around the country. It all made eminent sense, except that it still left a segment of moderate- and low-income families unable to afford housing.

From this sprang the realization that mortgage insurance alone could not assure adequate housing for all. Some forms of subsidies would be required to put roofs over their heads. At the same time, it became apparent that the viability of the FHA as an insurer might be compromised if its funds were to be used for anything but making good on delinquent mortgage loans. To remedy this shortcoming, Congress superimposed the Housing and Home Finance Agency atop the FHA and charged it with creating and supervising a bevy of new programs aimed at subsidizing housing for those least able to afford it on their own.

The government also came to recognize that many communities lacked the infrastructures to support all of this new housing. Decaying downtowns became inadequate for the growing communities. And so the government embarked on an ambitious program of urban renewal to aid communities in their efforts to revitalize their downtowns by guaranteeing loans and subsidizing certain phases of the redevelopment. It also made funds available for community facilities not needed heretofore. So all-encompassing did these activities become that they engendered the formation of the cabinet-level Department of Housing and Urban Development as their administrative center.

From a fairly simple home mortgage insurance program, self-financed and costing the taxpayers very little, the FHA grew into a mammoth bureaucracy that now disburses vast sums through a maze of housing ventures. In the process, demand for government assistance became so politicized that, to the surprise of no one, it has erupted into a series of scandals. The lesson to be learned is that government assistance and involvement feeds on itself to a point where the nation becomes dangerously dependent on public agencies for all but the most pedestrian needs and invites corruption as an inevitable concomitant.

None of this is to suggest that the nation erred by allowing the government to guarantee home mortgages and to participate, when absolutely necessary, in providing housing for the needy. Surely, there should be no homeless. And just as surely, the disadvantaged should not be relegated to substandard dwellings or left to the mercy of heartless landlords.

But if it took ingenuity to contrive the myriad government programs under which attractive shelter can be provided for millions, the same ingenuity should have been applied by the private sector without reliance on the public purse. The cost should be no greater since, in the final analysis, it is ultimately paid out of the taxpayers' wallet anyway. Admittedly, there have been some highly successful projects placed on the map by private interests with minimal government involvement, such as by the Partnership for Housing. They proved it can be done.

Housing is but one example of the countless government programs that feed the public illusion of getting something for nothing. There are grants, subsidies and loan guarantees available for virtually anything ranging from health care centers to museums. Never mind that none of this largess is free since every nickel is ultimately paid by the taxpayers. What weakens the national fiber is the indolence that results from reliance on some amorphous provenance.

So pernicious has this reliance become that it has reshaped the very concepts of leadership. Where once leaders were distinguished by their ability to mobilize the public into a constructive force for accomplishing a tangible goal, today's qualification for a leader is his ability to organize a march on Washington. Today, when a community organization seeks to employ an executive director, his most important asset is his knowledge of the myriad programs under which as many activities as possible can be funded. A prolific pen stroked across application forms and a keen understanding of the bureaucracy have become a mark of leadership.

Reliance on government paternalism need not entail direct fiscal assistance. Consider the pervasive regulation of business that became thoroughly entrenched since the Depression and World War II. Indeed, it goes back to the beginning of the century when the Sherman Antitrust Act first bore down on what then passed for mammoth corporate empires. Monopoly is somehow repugnant to the American mind in that it has the ability to extract unconscionable prices from a powerless consumer. But it becomes a value judgment to distinguish between monopolistic practices and economies of scale. The latter benefits the consumer in that it enables a large manufacturer to produce at lower unit costs and pass the saving along to the consumer. But the American consumer wants it both ways. On the one hand, he exhibits a ravenous appetite for new, convenient products at rock-bottom prices. On the other hand, he is dogged by a paranoia that thirsts to undo the very entities able to satisfy this appetite. He rails against what he perceives as tax loopholes for big corporations—tax incentives to spur research and development as well as to help finance mass-production of the goods he wants—while frowardly marching out of the marketplace with those very products in his shopping cart.

Who would have thought that the company that gave us most of the basic tools for communications in the computer age would wind up in the dock, accused of illegal monopolistic practices. If, as charged, Microsoft preyed on competitors in its climb to primacy in its field, it harmed neither the consumer public nor the country as a whole. With the negotiating skill of its management, surely negotiated remedies could have been found before the issue triggered legal action and the implied defamation of the pioneers who created the company.

The quest to get something for nothing is not limited to freeloading from the government. One amusing side of it can be found in the excesses worked by frequent fliers to skew what was intended to be an ingenious marketing program. Airlines, anxious to cultivate loyal followings, offered bonuses to those who patronized them on a regular basis. Fly enough miles and you are entitled to a free flight or to first-class seating on a coach ticket. Predictably, the airlines curried the favor of business travelers because it is they who fly most regularly on the same line's routes. It need not have concerned the airlines that these passengers' fares are usually paid by their employers so that, in effect, the traveler chooses the carrier and earns the bonus while his boss pays the bill. If this were not enough, stories abound of business travelers devising circuitous routes in order to amass bonus mileage while their employers try to find ways to gain control of those bonus miles for which they paid in the first place.

While this cat-and-mouse game seems harmless enough, it is indicative of some sorely misdirected energies. Appeals to the something-for-nothing psychology can be found in all sorts of advertising schemes and, what is worse, being accepted at face value by those who are always ready for a free lunch. Rebates and low-interest loans are offered to sway buyers of automobiles and other goods who seem blithely unaware—who really want to be unaware—of the fact that they are paying for the redundantly labeled "free gifts" elsewhere in the sticker price.

The same is true of the wide range of benefits offered by employers to their work forces. They had their origins in the actuarial discovery by providers of health insurance that hospital and surgical coverage can be provided at substantially lower premiums when entire groups of workers are insured. This spreading of the risk could be conveniently arranged when an employer's entire work force—some in robust health and others prone to ailments—is included in a group policy. In its earliest form, such health insurance was made available to employees at their own cost with the explication that group coverage was far cheaper than individual policies and with the admonition that no responsible breadwinner should be without some sort of health insurance. In time, employers bent to the demands of their workers that health-insurance premiums should become part of the compensation package. Since the same principle applied to life insurance, this, too, found its way into employee benefit programs. So did tuition assistance, charitable gift-matching and a host of other benefit programs, not to mention the most basic of all—pensions. If employees were aware that the cost of these benefits was reflected elsewhere in the labor-cost ledger, they cheerfully looked the other way. The cold fact is, however, that the direct cost and the administrative expenses of such benefit packages can run into hundreds of millions a year in a large corporation and into meaningful numbers of dollars for even a small employer.

In a recent strike situation, an employee on the picket line allowed as to how all this suddenly dawned on him. In that particular strike, the bone of contention was the company's insistence on shifting the cost of medical insurance back to the employees. Out on the sidewalk, this striker came to realize that he and his fellow workers had forgone larger wage increases in past years in order to secure the health-care package free of charge; that, in effect, he had been paying for it all along by leaving some of the proffered raises in the employer's hands, to be used to pay the medical premiums. It seemed a rude awakening for one who had grown accustomed to letting his employer pay his bills—accustomed to a free lunch.

None of this should be taken as a condemnation of group health-care and life insurance for employees, of tuition assistance, or of pension plans. They meet a vital need and make economic sense. But they should be recognized for what they are. People are paid for the work they perform, and modern society demands they be paid fairly and, if possible, generously. If employees choose to delegate their employers as their agents in such matters as insurance, investment of savings for retirement or financial planning for their children's education, they should be cognizant of what they have done. All too often, however, employees regard the benefit package as manna from heaven and would rather not think about who pays the piper.

Such abdication of responsibility weakens the American fabric. The muscles that make decisions become flabby and, faced with a national crisis, we become hard-put to make the difficult choices imposed on us. Self-reliance was at the root of a nation that clawed its way from colonial subservience to the mightiest economic and military power on earth. To relinquish it means to relinquish our fate to the will of others.

MAKING CHOICES II

No nation has been endowed with a better blueprint for managing its affairs than the United States. So near-perfect is the framework of the Constitution that, over two centuries, it has been materially changed only about a dozen times. It has served as a matrix for any number of other countries in structuring their own republics. But for all its grandeur and precision, the Constitution is very much like a do-it-yourself set of instructions for assembling an intricate apparatus. It leaves to those who implement it the choice of tightening all the nuts and bolts with great care or doing it in slap-dash haste. It places few firm restrictions on how to embellish the finished apparatus with accessories that serve special needs, nor does it preclude its misuse in the hands of the inept or ill-intentioned.

Logic tells us that the framers of the Constitution knew this full well. Their own turbulent era taught them that history is not static and that a living Constitution may need adjustments to be relevant in years beyond their powers to foresee. Wisely, they provided for the amendment process. They recognized that no combination of words, no matter how carefully chosen, can always mean the same thing to all people. Consequently, they charged the judicial branch of the government with the task of interpreting their words as they apply to an infinite combination of situations that might arise as the nation develops. They understood the meaning of flexibility and the right of people to make choices. Indeed, it was the proscription against free choice in their own countries that prompted the early settlers to come to America, to be followed by generations of immigrants who left their homelands for the same reason.

What the framers could not have predicted is the paralysis that has recently seized Americans in making the difficult choices. Not the easy choices from among candidates for public office; nor the desultory choice of letting a cadre of activists fill the vacuum created by popular abdication from hands-on citizenship. Hands-on citizenship is more than griping, more than turning the rascals out when things go awry, more than opting for new institutions when the old ones seem unsatisfactory. It does mean taking part in the formulation of contemporary thought and its translation into the processes of government. When Lincoln included government "by the people" in his triptych of freedom, he apparently had more than the ballot in mind.

Nothing in the Constitution instructs us in the fine art of making choices. It merely hints at the choices to be made and provides us with the parameters of our options. Beyond that, we are on our own.

As one example of this flexibility, the Constitution prescribes the prerequisites for holding public office and stewarding the public trust. But it is silent on the personalities best suited to carry out such public duties, and for good reason. The framers remembered all too well the miscarriages that could ensue when absolute power is conferred on a ruling dynasty or when a cabal usurps that power without prior qualifications to rule. In their wisdom, they refrained from defining the personal qualities and experiences that render potential candidates viable for public office. Nor did they—nor could they—devise a litmus test for the motives that propel aspirants into the political arena. It is one of the difficult choices they left to the people.

By and large, we have been fortunate in that the vast majority of office holders at all levels of government embarked on their political careers with what, to them at least, were honorable motives. We are lucky, also, in that the hidden agendas of most miscreants were ultimately exposed and that, hopefully, some lessons were learned each time malfeasance came to light. But we have yet to make that difficult choice of who it is we really want to lead us while we look away and pursue our own daily lives.

In renouncing the opportunity to ascend a throne, George Washington did more than abjure an American monarchy. He also signaled that high places of power should not be reserved for the highborn. And, indeed, our office holders through two centuries and at every level have come from virtually every stratum of society. However, this is more to be attributed to ad hoc selections than to a deliberate choice made by the people as to who should lead them. This kind of ambivalence has come to haunt us, however, as, time and again, the government's energies are diverted as it roots around for evidence of malfeasance and worse. In fact, this witch-hunting has become an obsession, fueled by the media and tolerated by a gullible public that equates paranoia with vigilance. Witness only the Senate confirmation hearings on the nominations of Robert Bork and John Tower.

Basic honesty notwithstanding, what are we to expect of the people who offer themselves, yea strive mightily, for public office? Say what you will, there is a difference of approach between those who make politics an income-producing career and those who regard it as noblesse oblige. The fact that some of our finest statesmen have come from the ranks of the working class and some of our dimmer lights from moneyed backgrounds proves nothing, and the obverse has little meaning, either. This is only proper in a nation that has forsworn aristocracy and a class system. But this does not mean that the two groups are alike in their concepts of public office.

Follow the investigations into official impropriety and you will almost always find that they turn on money. In broad terms, there are two basic scenarios. The most common scenario finds the suspect officer holder discovering along the way that his public duties also offer opportunities to accumulate some measure of wealth that seemed inaccessible in private life. This is not to say that this was his primary motive for entering politics, but rather that temptation is greater for those whose backgrounds had previously denied them financial security. In the second scenario, office holders from affluent backgrounds are vulnerable to the temptation of favoring their wealthy friends in the discharge of their duties, in the legislation they sponsor and the policies they advocate.

Of course, this is not universally true by any means. Some of this nation's greatest leaders came from modest backgrounds, grew into giants and did not have a dishonest bone in their bodies. By the same token, some who came from patrician families were vocal and effective champions of the underprivileged.

But the fact remains that we, as a people, have failed to come to grips with the basic choice of what qualifies a person for leadership. Rather, we rely on the political parties to present us with candidates, attractively groomed and neatly packaged. This is not a choice. If it were, we would have no right to complain when a member of Congress is charged with supplementing his income with questionable honoraria or accepting financial interest in a company doing business with the government, possibly through his intervention. If it were, we would have no right to be shocked when an official pursues policies that favor the well-to-do. If it were a matter of choice, we should have taken such proclivities into consideration before entrusting the reins of government to them.

This is not advocacy of a government either by plutocrats or by commoners. Rather it is a warning that the choice has to be made, unwelcome as it may be. If we fail to make it, the innate strength of our public trust will become mired in a morass of recriminations. We hear them now. When Lyndon Johnson spent freely on his New Society programs to improve the lot of the distressed, those affronted by all the largess wondered aloud whether the U.S. is headed for some form of socialism. And when Ronald Reagan dismantled or curtailed many of the socially-oriented spending programs, cries arose about insensitivity and favor-the-rich cronyism.

If we were to make a clear choice, we would have two options to consider. Is it the government's function to sustain those of our citizens who cannot sustain themselves? Or is it a proper role for the government to ease the way for those—call them the rich—whose industry enables people to sustain themselves through increased employment? This choice, if we ever muster the gumption to make it, will determine the profile of our future leadership. We cannot afford to postpone that choice.

Just as urgent is our need to make a clear decision on interracial relations. We cannot long continue to wear the blinders that shield the privileged few from the ugliness of racial strife, often bloody, that results from discrimination. This is a choice we cannot abdicate to government. Regulation of attitudes is not within government's purview.

No amount of government intervention can solve the problems of racial hatred. True, the emancipation of slaves was a milestone, but is it thinkable that Lincoln could have acted otherwise had the slaves been white? Or would the poll tax have long survived, even if it had not been directed primarily at Negroes? Laws to enforce equal employment and housing opportunities have certainly benefited those of African descent and, with them, other minorities that suffer from discrimination. But laws can be circumvented, and often are. They are being circumvented by those who refuse to regard people of races other than their own as their equals. And as long as such biased attitudes persist, the problem of race relations cannot be solved. Government cannot do it. It is a choice the people have to make, no matter how distasteful it may seem to some.

Let us be clear about one aspect of that choice. It is not a racial option. This becomes apparent when we consider our ambivalence about Blacks, Hispanics or sometimes even Asians. It is not uncommon for Whites to work in close harmony and mutual respect with minority colleagues and, at the same time, abhor those same minorities in a social context. The bias here is not against the color of their skin but against their economic status and lack of education and social breeding. Admittedly, lack of education and social graces are the consequences of deprivation caused by centuries of racial discrimination, but recognition of the cause alone does little to heal the social rifts. Failing to understand this distinction leads to disintegration of our precepts of government and justice. How often has it been said that Blacks receive harsher judgment before the bar than do Whites. And conversely, how often do we hear that the law favors minorities in an exaggerated effort to appear evenhanded. Either way, the concept of equal justice for all is compromised and with it one of the pillars of our republic.

Perhaps the concept of America as a melting pot has become obsolete and ill serves us. It implies that we are a conglomeration of incompatible races and cultures whose differences survive eternally. So long as these differences remain in our consciousness, racial and ethnic prejudices will also perpetuate themselves. If we are serious about racial equality, we must accept the fact that Americans are a race unto itself, one that reproduces itself in a variety of skin tones and other characteristics. While the designation of Indians was a misnomer from the beginning, the current vogue of calling them Native Americans serves only to suggest that others born on American soil or of American parents are not native Americans.

The choice we really have to make is whether this country can long flourish while it continues to recognize an underclass. If we, indeed, permit racial minorities to exist as an underclass, we must also assume the obligations that an underclass imposes on a society. These obligations played a role in the undoing of many civilizations that divided their populations along such lines. What undid them was the growing need by a relatively small ruling class to shoulder responsibility for their serfs who outnumbered them and whom they did not trust to shift for themselves—in fact, did not trust at all. We are in danger of doing the same and that way lies disaster.

One danger is that the underclass status has a certain appeal for those who become increasingly convinced that society owes them something. In fact, leaders of minority causes are already making a handsome living from spreading that gospel. In the end, we may wind up bankrupting ourselves, as have previous civilizations, by shouldering the financial burden of supporting an underclass that could be fully capable of fending for itself if we but gave them the opportunity and free access to the perquisites of such independence. Finally, we are depriving ourselves of the productivity and managerial contribution these minorities could make to our economy rather than sap its strength through the vast array of support programs put in place to assuage our indecision and guilt.

If, on the other hand, we choose to give the underclass syndrome a decent burial, we must do this as a people and not in reliance on government programs, no matter how well-intentioned. Laws are not substitutes for attitudes, and it is our attitude that is at the core of this choice. This may be a bitter choice for those whose traditions are based on outdated prejudices, and even for those who, despite their best intentions, cannot account for their xenophobia.

Eliminating the underclass concept will not solve all our problems, because a free society has yet to find an alternative to financial and social inequality. Nor am I certain that it should. Not even the so-called Communist nations have been able to attain anything near such equality, and they are finally giving voice to this recognition. By personal savvy, by tenacity, by being in the right place at the right time, some among us will always enjoy the fruits of success while others sweat and strain to keep body and soul together. Whether success is expressed in terms of wealth or of bureaucratic privilege is immaterial. There will always be menial tasks to be performed and those to whom they fall will not enjoy the same degree of luxury as those who employ them and take the risks. But race or ethnic origin should have nothing to do with it if we are to step off the treadmill that perpetuates the cost of subsidizing an underclass.

It would be hard to separate a discussion of an underclass from the subculture that the drug scourge has forced upon us. Here, too, difficult choices are eluding us. Make no mistake about it, the two are related. There is nothing new about the use of cocaine and other addictive substances. At an earlier time, however, they were the opiates of the jaded rich and the artistic world. A few sophisticates knew how to handle drugs, others became sorry victims of the habit. Today's drug scene is different. It has gripped the underclass in its search for liberation from despair but, instead, has engulfed its victims in the quicksand of hopelessness. Ironically, it has also given some of the more disadvantaged their first taste of enterprise by turning them into dealers. True, some of the upwardly mobile have also succumbed to occasional sniffing and worse. But, for them, drugs are an ill-chosen answer to social and business pressures when martinis can no longer do the job. For a time, at least, they are able to afford their habits and so they manage to escape the subculture that tugs at their coattails until either they mend their ways or fall into the abyss.

A nation befogged by life in a spreading haze of intoxication has nowhere to go. And while drug addicts still constitute a small minority of the population as a whole, nobody in control of his senses disagrees with the need to do something. But the difficult choices have yet to be made.

Exhortations to say no to drugs, arrests, seizures of illegal substances and rehabilitation clinics for the addicted are part of the solution, but they evade the real decisions that will have to be made if we are to banish drugs from the American scene. The choice before us: whom do we propose to protect?

Until now, the emphasis has been on dealing with users and those who supply them. Police raids and border patrols interdict some small part of the market. Employers are taught to ferret out users and find counsel for them on kicking the habit. The power of criminal justice has been enlisted to take both users and dealers off the streets with only modest success. And still there is blood on the sidewalks of our urban centers, and there are neighborhoods where residents are afraid to walk at night for fear of being caught in the crossfire.

When will we face the cruel choice of protecting the nonusers first, even at the risk of consigning a generation of addicts to the junk heap of society? It is an excruciating choice, but one that must be made. And none of our responses to the problem have taken that direction.

Interdiction of drugs may sound noble but it serves only to diminish the supply even as demand keeps growing. Simple economics dictate that a shrinking supply raises the price of drugs, rendering more of the addicted desperate enough to resort to crime in order to obtain their fix. Curtailed supplies will also enhance the role of the dealers and their overlords to a point where bullets become the coin of the realm. Have we learned nothing from Prohibition? By facetious contrast, imagine a six-pack of crack vials on the supermarket shelf for sixty cents. Those reckless enough to indulge could buy it with impunity and without resorting to dishonesty. And just as it would be hard to imagine gunfire among rival suppliers of baked beans, so would there be no bloody franchise in the drug trade.

To be serious about it, the hooked user will continue to succumb whether he can buy the stuff cheaply from the store shelf or must hold up a gasoline station, kill the proprietor and clean out the till to support his habit. That crack has a lower price tag than, say, heroin only serves to point up the futility of trying to save the addicted. Go shopping for a $14 bottle of Scotch in your neighborhood liquor store and you are bound to see a wino stumble in for his $1 pint of Sneaky Pete. He is beyond retrieve and price has nothing to do with it. Drug rehabilitation clinics should open their doors to anyone genuinely wanting to kick the habit. It may be a good investment for taxpayers to fund such clinics.

Clearly some addicts want to rejoin the nonusers whose protection a courageous choice would make our first priority.

In a loftier realm, we continue to wallow in ambivalence about what, for lack of a better term, we call separation of church and state. The framers of the Constitution did not call it that, though they did ordain in the Bill of Rights that this nation shall not establish a state religion. There is a difference. To our Founding Fathers the tyranny of a state religion was fresh in the mind. They resolved not to let it happen here though they could not have foreseen its unlikelihood in a nation of 200 million people from hundreds of ethnic origins. Their principle was sound. Their statement was firm enough. It is we who, in the name of religious freedom, relegate to the courts the decisions we should be making. As a result, such policies as we now have turn solely on the issue of constitutionality, i.e., whether any given act violates the proscription in the Bill of Rights.

Does a crèche or a menorah in front of City Hall threaten to impose a state religion? Does a moment of silence or silent prayer at the beginning of the school day open the gates to religious tyranny? Such symbolism may offend some of our citizens, but their abolition offends others.

Clearly, the Framers' purpose was not to please everybody, but rather to close the door on a particular impediment to freedom. What we are doing, however, is paving the way to state-sponsored anti-religionism. So frightened are we of any official concurrence in religious practices that we are prepared to sacrifice some of the most solemn rites on the altar of religious freedom.

Would freedom be any more secure if the President no longer lighted the national Christmas tree on the White House lawn, or if he were obligated to kindle a menorah next to it? Does a mayor of New York compromise religious freedom by marching in the St. Patrick's Day parade one day and donning a yarmulke the next for a visit to a Brooklyn synagogue?

What the framers of the Constitution were really saying is that religion is a highly personal conviction and its choice is to be left to individuals. They said nothing about the trappings, and for good reason. The trappings are public symbols that identify adherents of the same faith to each other and to the community at large. Unquestionably, numbers play a role in all this. Since the vast majority of Americans are Christians of various persuasions, it is more likely that lighted trees would grace the portals of public buildings and less likely that a Buddha would appear on the White House lawn on the Tet holiday. This does not connote that officialdom means to root out Buddhism in America or impose Christianity on all Americans.

Religious tyranny has never resulted from popular demand. Rather, it was spawned by tyrants to consolidate their power by foisting a state religion on a populace that feared deity more than a temporal ruler and then succumbed by outdoing itself to implement his devilish fiat. Lest I be accused of having a short memory, let me add that the Holocaust, for all its unspeakable horror, was not a case of establishing a German state religion. Jews in Nazi Germany were never given the option of converting to a state-sanctioned religion in order to escape persecution. Quite the contrary, those who had previously accepted baptism, for whatever reason, were not immune to the atrocities nor were their descendants who, for all practical purposes, were born Christians. Aryan purity, in whose name Hitler set upon Jews and other religious and ethnic groups, was not a religion at all nor is there any certainty that Hitler, himself, was an Aryan or even understood the term's meaning.

The choice before us is the degree to which Americans will allow a clear and simple Constitutional guarantee to inhibit pursuit of their religious creeds under the auspices of a government that already subscribes to godliness in virtually its every act. "Good night and God bless you," is the customary sign-off of a Presidential speech. Even atheists are content to spend currency that says "In God We Trust." The truth is that a state religion, of whatever denomination, would not be tolerated by the very people with the power to establish it. No politician could function freely if, in the end, he would have to answer to a religious prelate, be it an archbishop or ayatollah. Or even the Pope. We proved that with the election of John F. Kennedy who, though devoutly Catholic, clearly was not of a mind to cede his powers to another authority. If the government, which we freely elect, openly endorses the moral precepts that all religions teach, it bespeaks religious freedom, not tyranny.

If we come close to anything approaching religious tyranny, it is on the issue of abortion. It is here that Americans confuse religion with morality. They are not the same. You can be moral without being religious, but it is hypocrisy to profess religiousness when you are immoral. On its surface, abortion does seem to be a religious issue in that its strongest opposition comes from the Catholic church and some fundamentalist sects whose doctrines forbid any intentional interference with procreation. The validity of their views must not be challenged for it stems from the sanctity of their beliefs and their inalienable right to hold them. Whether all of their communicants share those beliefs or choose to follow their dictates is not to the point. By and large, those with less stringent religious affiliations, and those with none at all, appear to be in the forefront of free-choice advocates. While this is more than coincidence, we should not be drawn into a pissing contest over whose religion is more to be respected.

In order to avoid the hard choices concerning abortion we invent specious issues. Does life begin at conception or when the fetus is viable outside the womb or after birth? Is a woman's body her exclusive province and possibly that of her husband or doctor? Who cares? Answers to these questions can be used to advocate pro- or anti- abortion positions, and they are.

No matter when life is said to begin, a truly religious stand would be to deny the right of any person to thwart the will of God. If, therefore, it is God's will that a child be born of any given union, of whatever marital status, then that child should be brought into the world. This view must also preclude reliance on birth control or even abstinence. But that would mean questioning the omnipotence of God, within whose power it also is to provide a condom at a convenient time and place, or to give the fertile bride a sudden headache during her husband's concupiscence. Agnostics have no such problem since they do not acknowledge a deity. Clearly, then, abortion is not a religious issue. If it were and if anti-abortion laws were to prevail, we should truly fear that state religion has stuck its nose under our tent.

Perhaps, the issue is an ethical one. The ethics of subjecting an unwanted child to a life fraught with disadvantage from birth, all for the release of sexual tension, are far more compelling. So are the ethics of eschewing the joys—and tribulations—of parenthood for the sake of an often transitory career advantage, especially when all other conditions favor launching a new life in comfort and privilege. And ethics play no role at all in subsidizing an unwed woman in promiscuous child-bearing when she should be working.

Rather than confront these issues, we find scapegoats. The so-called sexual liberation of the 1960's is one. Another is surrender to the elitist shibboleth that the poor have nothing better to do with their time than to fornicate, and it is therefore humane to abet them with welfare programs.

To rail on religious grounds against the sexual promiscuity spawned by the 1960's is hypocritical. The Judeo-Christian faiths are rooted in a culture that condoned polygamy. Islam still does. And concubinage, though little practiced, is part and parcel of Oriental cultures. The big difference is that these ancients indulged their passions in full awareness of the responsibility they bore toward their offspring.

Responsibility, then, is the real issue of abortion. No religion, no cult of do-gooders, least of all the government, should usurp the right of Americans to decide how they cope with their libidos so long as they are on notice that no one will free them from the burdens of parenthood—before or after birth. If rape, incest or a mother's fragile health make it inadvisable—even immoral—to carry to full term, these contingencies should be treated as medical problems, with government help offered only to the extent that we choose generally to make government the custodian of our well-being. A tough choice? Maybe. But one we cannot elude.

Why is it vital that Americans, as a people, make clear choices such as these and many others? While pluralism has its role in a free, democratic society, there is also a need for a greater amount of cohesion than we have been able to muster, certainly in the second half of the last century. We find ourselves at a loss whenever we are confronted by foes whose single-mindedness—in military or industrial competition—threatens to overtake us while we bicker. This is not to say their single-mindedness may not be misdirected or even born of free choice. Indeed, our most potent enemies have been dictatorships where single-mindedness is imposed on the people. Freely chosen or not, consensus is a formidable tool in the hands of a nation. Consensus and pluralism are not mutually exclusive, however. In fact, they can work synergistically for free men and women in forming national policies. But, once established, such policies must be implemented without distractions.

Is it credible that, in a time of countless challenges confronting us, our national legislature can devote endless days to debating whether one of their number profited from an involvement with a commercial entity or used his position to gain some other advantage after his term of office? Such transgressions—and they will recur as long as we set no rigid standards that qualify a candidate for the political arena—should be foreclosed by a national consensus on what constitutes eligibility for leadership, beginning at the lowest municipal level. We are capable of devising tests to determine who should be college bound, but we seem unable to judge in advance the qualifications of an aspirant to public office or his viability when he gets there.

We may well have the best-developed judicial system of any nation in the world. Yet we clog it with forensics to decide matters that the people should have the visceral fortitude to settle. Race relations is a clear example. Discrimination in employment, housing and education become an issue for the courts solely because we, as a people, have failed to make the choice on an equality that should be self-evident to us all. We proclaim religious freedom one moment and the next file briefs to impinge on it with trivialities. Meanwhile, the serious questions on which consensus is not readily attainable molder under the backlog of cases that burden our network of courts. To make matters worse, we regard judgeships as the highest priesthood of the legal profession and, at the same time, refuse to remunerate judges adequately, forcing many to leave the bench and relinquish their seats to political strivers in search of a meal ticket.

Our self-divisiveness, in the name of pluralism, is mirrored in the media. There is hardly a day when the television screen does not bristle with demonstrations for or against a cause or when some officeholder is not shown on the road to political crucifixion. Given the same images from a country less stable than ours, observers would be quick to tell us that a revolution was brewing. Of course, most of our demonstrations are peaceful and restrained, and revolt against the system is furthest from our minds. Charitably, they are akin to family squabbles, and we do have an enormous capacity for kissing and making up. But this does not alter the fact that, like in a family given to bickering, our national skin turns raw at times and diverts our attention from the pursuit of the greatness we habitually profess for our nation.

Were that we could be as determined in our pursuit of national greatness as we are of the goals that divide us. Unity on the major conduct of our national life is within our grasp, if we but make the choices to attain it.

Taking Risks II

From the moment the first settlers set sail for America, risk was their constant companion. Little does it matter that most were escaping danger and privation at their points of origin as well. Whatever drove them to their journey to the unknown, across a furious sea, they knew that the security they envisioned would have to be attained at great peril. They were not to be disappointed. A crude environment and hostile natives were only the beginning. With them the settlers brought some of the baggage they had hoped to shed as the tyranny of their homelands followed them in the form of royal overseers who sought to spread empire to the colonies. They were forced to fight cruel wars and countless skirmishes before their independence was vouchsafed.

Their motivation was not negative, however. It was not merely an exodus from states that were intolerable. More emphatically, it was a venture to create for themselves and their descendants a new life that, within the limits of their vision in those times, required virgin territory to give them free rein over their destiny. There would be false starts and missteps. Some took to hankering for a return to the devil they knew when the obstacles seemed insurmountable, and a few even turned renegades in the final showdown. In the process, they learned the lesson every mountain climber takes to heart: once half-way up the escarpment, it is as risky to turn back as it is to continue climbing.

Their courage and that of those who followed was rewarded. Different times produced different risks, but if America's majesty can be attributed to any one trait, it was the ability of its people to look uncertainty in the face and stare it down. So strong was our people's determination to succeed in everything they attempted that they were able to sweep the doubters and fainthearted with them in their march to greatness.

By now it should be axiomatic that risk comes with the territory when you aspire to lofty goals, but that truism seems to elude us of late as we increasingly look to protect our backsides in every facet of national and individual life. That bespeaks a geriatric view of our country. As my father grew old in financial comfort, he once remarked that he no longer needed to make any money but he could not afford to risk losing any of it. A sensible outlook for someone contemplating the home stretch. But is America in the home stretch? Is this the best we can hold out for our children and the generations they hope to raise? If so, I should be glad that my days, too, are numbered. It is odd, then, that other nations, both large and just emerging, should be striving to emulate our past performance by assuming risks we are no longer willing to shoulder.

The risks taken by the Solidarity movement in Poland are inspiring. Faced with danger of imprisonment and possibly crushing intervention by the Soviet mentors of the Communist dictatorship, its leaders plowed ahead on a road that, in many ways, would have been familiar to the founders of the United States. Around the world, peoples are throwing caution to the winds in their pursuit of principles that have worked for America. And as they do, we rest on the laurels we bravely earned over five centuries and hoped to secure at staggering human cost in two world wars. Perhaps, after successful struggle, it seems only right to indulge one's comfort and catch one's breath. But, in a race, even a well-deserved respite invites the possibility of being overtaken. Human endeavor is, indeed, an unending race for supremacy and its rewards whose only finish line can be the achievement of Utopia.

Therefore, risk is inevitable—even for us. As the growing industrial powers, some of them deprived of ready access to fossil fuels, turn to nuclear power—an American discovery, at that—to reach higher economic plateaus, we treat it like an infernal contraption. Only nuclear scientists can fairly spell out the risks of a contained accident or even a dreaded meltdown. As in any pioneering venture, there could be human and material loss. But the alternative is even riskier. Whatever its dimensions, the world's supply of hydrocarbons is limited and its last vestiges will be found in countries whose affections for us are questionable at best. While we debate and demonstrate over the evacuation of a few citizens from the ten miles surrounding a proposed nuclear power plant in case of a mishap—which, with current technology, need never happen—we may find ourselves held hostage by potentates whose plans for our future are thoroughly uninviting. There are alternatives, to be sure. Conversion of other natural resources to usable energy requires heavy investment in research and experimentation and environmental compromises we are also loath to make. Either way, we must take risks to secure our energy prospects. And the way to take them is to forswear our silly diddling with exotic toys that may extract an occasional spark from the wind, the sea, human refuse—even the sun. The real answer lies in the cosmic power of the atom and we have already harnessed it. Let us use it.

Whichever way we propose to fuel our future, it will have an effect on our environment. This, too, is a risk we cannot shirk. It is not too brash to suggest that from the moment man was placed on earth, he has despoiled the environment in one way or another. He hunted animals for food and pelts and endangered many species. He has cut and burned forests to free himself from hunger and cold. He has dumped detritus in every direction and polluted air and water with every foul excrement of life as it evolved through the millennia. And still the earth is predominantly green, the ocean blue and the air oxygen-laden enough to support life. It may be that we failed to understand the risks we took with our environment when we embarked on the growth that has marked this nation's history. We could not have been totally blind to the smoke that belched from our factories and locomotives. It could not have looked cleaner to our forebears than it does to us. But they braved the risks in their unquenchable desire to get things done. If modern science now teaches us about the malignant ingredients of industrial smoke and of the by-products we discard as part of daily life, all well and good so long as we accept them as part of the risk of progress. If, in addition, modern technology can show us the way to safer waste disposal, less polluting manufacturing processes and better protection of our natural assets, we should welcome its contribution. There is no sense in trampling callously on the beauty of our land or abusing our habitat.

Nevertheless, if we fail to accept the risks of progress as did our forefathers, we are doomed to stagnation that, in the end, may ravage the land even more drastically. We can see this in the ghost towns that resulted when economic collapse stopped progress. For years we could see it in the abandoned mill communities of New England until new industries moved in to rejuvenate them. Despair begets neglect, and neglect can be more deleterious even than controlled abuse. A kitchen that is messy after cooking a sumptuous meal is preferable to the pantry of a patient too sick to eat.

And so it is with our personal lives. We speak endlessly of our good fortune in being, for the most part, a healthy, well-nourished society. This is largely the result of the richness of our land and all that grows on it. If ours has not been the world's finest cuisine, as connoisseurs might tell us, it has certainly been rich in the nutrients that made some of us strong and the rest of us fat. But with this cornucopia has come a sense of contentment and confidence that spurred us on to greater heights. Now, of a sudden, we shrink from this bounty as though it were poison. We waste countless hours and calories attending to our bodies as if their preservation were our chief mission in life. So pervasive is our concern with avoiding the risks of living that we misdirect our energies.

It was not so long ago that we hailed the demise of the 12-hour work day that required us to rise before dawn. We still greet the sun on our feet, but now it is on running paths where we sap our energy before we even begin to be productive. And then we wonder why the Japanese, who also rise before dawn, put us to shame with their productivity and resourcefulness. Come the end of the day, we turn to contemplating our navels over vegetable juice and noncaloric dips while, again, the Japanese go carousing with customers over booze and beer. And, again, we wonder what is causing our trade deficits.

The men and women who made this country great were largely a chain-smoking, hard-drinking lot who took their chances with the world they lived in. They took risk and adversity in stride, knowing that the risks and adversities of failure were even more ominous. When they read, they read for learning or pleasure, not for hints on how to keep their gall bladders happy. When they drank, they drank for conviviality and a sense of ease, not to keep their urinary tracts lubricated. And when they smoked, it gave them an air of luxury without concern for what it might do to their lungs or the air they breathed. Not only did they survive; they triumphed over the fears that, given our sheltered existence, cause us to shrink into the grave ungratified.

They had a zest for living that we somehow have lost. They had a talent for taking risks from which we instinctively recoil. They put illness, injury and death into proper perspective and gained something in the bargain. By contrast, we take our risks vicariously. Never before have gore and incredible risks been more popular in screen entertainment than they are now. Dizzying car chases and superhuman combat can be viewed from the safe havens of the couch or theater seat and in the knowledge that such adventures cannot take any skin off our noses. There is something inherently wrong with all that. For one thing, it enables us to conjure up courage that we actually lack. We could not tolerate watching such carnage were it not for the fall-back assurance that we are seeing stunt-men oozing ketchup. For another, it gives us an exaggerated view of the risks that even a courageous life normally imposes on us and thereby teaches us that the way of sanity is to avoid all risks scrupulously. There is no gainsaying the real horrors of war, but our portrayal of them turns heroic patriots into Rambo-like monsters for no discernible purpose except to gratify. Most of all, such vicariousness dulls our sense for judging the risk-to-reward ratio of real-life situations. This can be seen from the recklessness of street criminals who apparently equate the violent actions gleaned from the screen with their own capabilities.

To think we can attain absolute safety by sipping wine instead of downing a robust snort, by walking out of rooms where someone has the audacity to smoke, by nibbling on veggies while hardier souls feast on steak, cheese, deviled eggs and chopped liver is to enter a fool's paradise. While there, assuaging our guilt, we remain exposed to risks beyond our control. Platitudes notwithstanding, we will never be masters of our fate. A true appreciation of life and all it has to offer means to tackle the challenges over which we have at least some measure of mastery and by which we can enrich our own and others' inexorable march to our ultimate destiny.

In order to regain our forward momentum as a people, we must first recapture the equilibrium that enabled our forebears to take sensible risks without fear. We cannot make demands on life without offering something of our comfort and safety in return. We want, as a matter of routine, to be transported for pleasure or business from one end of the world to another in a matter of hours, but we refuse to accept the risks of streaking at nearly the speed of sound, six miles above the ground and at the tender mercies of mere mortals at the controls. Our lifestyle demands that there be at least one automobile in every driveway, but we are shocked that there should be human lapses in the design and manufacture of these cars by the millions. We demand a handy remedy for every discomfort but we become vindictive when one of them produces unwanted side-effects despite the best efforts of their human creators.

When occasionally we come face-to-face with the chances we have taken, we abdicate our responsibility for having taken them and deputize investigators or consumer advocates to scold not us, but those on whom they can conveniently—and to great applause—pin the blame. We must do better than that.

We must do better, also, in assuming the risks that devolve on us as citizens. Every time we cast a ballot, we must assume the risk of having made an unwise choice. Most certainly, we cannot delude ourselves into believing that, because a political party or candidate generally reflects our own views, the same regime will not, once elected, espouse some policy with which we disagree. Public officials are not our clones. To some degree, the Founding Fathers reduced these risks by incorporating checks and balances into our system of government. They provided, among other things, for the Senate's consent in the appointment of high-ranking officials and the ratification of treaties. However, their caution did not extend to the hamstringing of Presidents in assembling their administrations or in the conduct of those duties specifically assigned to the chief executive.

The spectacle of Senate hearings on matters best left to the executive—yea, specifically charged to him—has become an absurdity. Short of naming an outright rascal or incompetent to a sensitive government post, the President should be free to assemble his own team. And short of plunging the nation into war or an unconscionable alliance, the conduct of foreign policy was carefully ascribed to the presidency. Sure, this exposes us to some risks, and the framers of the Constitution knew it. But their measured precaution has been skewed to a point where, for all intents and purposes, we are just one step short of allowing a politically hostile Senate to make the appointments albeit, out of false courtesy, from a list of nominees offered by the President.

Much the same is true of the intrusion on domestic and foreign policy. In the name of monitoring these policies, Congressional investigations so beset the executive departments that they virtually paralyze administrators in the performance of their real tasks. True, something was amiss in what has become known as the Iran-Contra affair. While everybody seemed to agree that concourse with post-Shah Iran had reached a dangerous impasse and that the Sandinistas threatened to turn Central America into an enemy camp, the actions of a few super-patriots and power seekers in promoting an ex officio policy of their own was at best misguided and perhaps unlawful. Nevertheless, it can fairly be said that the election of a different President, while it might have prevented an Iran-Contra affair, might also have resulted in different, more grievous missteps. By the same token, there may be room for disagreement on whether Robert Bork was the optimum choice for the Supreme Court or John Tower for the Defense Department. Certainly, neither was the kind of miscreant the framers sought to keep out of office, and so long as they had the President's confidence, their ordeal before the Senate was an unwarranted intrusion on Presidential prerogative. Such are the risks entailed in free democratic behavior that not everybody can be promised his druthers when we make our choice.

Rather, it is a vibrant government apparatus that is at issue here. Snarled in a traffic jam of recriminations and suspicions, government cannot possibly discharge the duties for which taxpayers pay a heavy price. Call it foresight or determination, Franklin Roosevelt brooked no interference when he boldly and unilaterally conveyed fifty destroyers of the U.S. Navy to the British, an act that could conceivably have triggered a German declaration of war against us when we were ill-prepared. Just picture the hearings and special prosecutors, with Harry Hopkins in the dock, that would have ensued in today's environment. Simply put, we took a risk by electing Roosevelt and he, in turn, took a calculated risk to stave off a rout of the British and, with it, our ultimate involvement in the war. In the current context, Kennedy's misfired raid on the Bay of Pigs, Carter's failed rescue mission for the Iran hostages, and Reagan's invasion of Grenada and air raid on Libya warrant our admiration for their decisiveness regardless of their ultimate outcome or imperfect planning, to say nothing of Kennedy's firm response in the Cuban missile crisis. They were worthy of the American spirit.

Not so admirable is our lip service to the preservation of democratic freedom wherever it is threatened, followed by reluctance to take the necessary risks. We have, or at least should have, the most acutely tuned intelligence service of any nation, backed up by a clandestine strike force to carry out thrusts wherever freedom is threatened. Yet, more often than not, we waver when it comes to giving substance to our professions. We are still wracked by second thoughts about our deftness in removing Allende from power in Chile or revising the government of Guatemala. And we have refrained from drawing the stiletto at all against some of our tormentors in various parts of the world, offering the lame excuse that we cannot foster democratic behavior in other nations by using undemocratic means to do it. Wisely, we weigh the adverse consequences of the acts we contemplate, but such is the nature of assessing risk and reward. But we may be concentrating on the wrong risk. Is it really foreign reprisals that frighten our leaders, or the opportunity it gives the opposition party to earn brownie points with the voters by exposing the flaws that may have marred the exercise?

Finger-pointing is the province of the weak. When our policies go awry—as they must from time to time—all the people bear some responsibility. Monday-morning quarterbacking by those who have not shared in the decision-making process is neither courageous nor constructive, nor is the self-centered bravado of editorialists whose I-told-you-so wagging besmirches those who put their reputations on the line with every decision. Surely, we can do better than that.

Part of the answer may well lie in more focused dialogue on the risks of governing this land. It is incumbent on our elected officials to enumerate the risks when they spread out a proposed policy before the public. Are there risks in interdicting the drug trade's supply line? Of course there are. Are there risks in protecting the environment against all the inroads of industrial growth? Are there risks in guaranteeing every family a safety net in case of economic adversity? Indeed, are there risks in the complexity of a government that attempts to be all things to all people?

Risks there are, and we must either take them or forswear the demands we make on our country for absolute immunity to unhappiness. If we do neither, we are doomed to become an also-ran in the race of nations across the landscape of history.

Paying the Price

I refuse to believe that America has a death wish. The self-destruction our enemies wished on us at various times has not occurred, but the threat hangs over us nevertheless until we accept responsibility for the opportunities our land lavishes on us day by day. We are blessed with material riches and a plethora of human talent and wisdom, if we but avail ourselves of their promise. Bad choices are better than no choices at all. Risks offer hope of rewards. But security, peace, strength, growth and well-being all carry a hefty price tag. There is no free lunch. Death and taxes are not the only currency in the commerce of national glory.

Tolerance and understanding are on the bill if we are to buy our way to human dignity and equality. It is not enough to delegate our judges and law-givers to write intricate formulas by which minorities and the disadvantaged can gain reluctant acceptance into the mainstream of our society. The price is to relinquish often deep-seated prejudices and hatreds. The privileged must learn to budget their sense of superiority by recognizing that in which they are truly superior and that which they arrogate to themselves merely to buttress their position. There can be no underclass in a strong, vibrant society. It breeds struggle and diversion from loftier goals whenever energy that should be focused on progress and prosperity is squandered on racial and ethnic divisiveness. This is not to say that there cannot be—and will not be—various levels of economic ease. They cannot be eliminated in a society that prides itself on the freedom of all to strive according to their talents and capabilities and even to enjoy the heritage of wealth. There will be the rich, the poor and those in between in a free economy.

Tolerance and understanding, however, are not enough. The price of freedom also includes the cost of taking responsibility for the needy such an economy inevitably spawns. We are paying that price now in the form of taxes to defray the myriad entitlement programs and the hordes that implement them. How much cheaper it might be for those with the means to assume that responsibility themselves. Our laws discourage it now. Under our present tax code, a contribution to the National Association for Ingrown Toenails is deductible from taxable income. An outright gift to a distressed family in the neighborhood is not.

There is nobility in voluntarily sharing our wealth with the poor, with worthy institutions that provide solace, healing, education and cultural enrichment. While government programs devise rigid standards to govern its grants and subsidies, ostensibly to prevent abuse but more likely to winnow out the growing list of supplicants, we, as individuals, would be free to pick and choose beneficiaries according to our hearts' dictates. Given the diversity of human feelings in such matters, the distribution of largess would be equitable. And at less cost. Tithing has fallen by the wayside as a measure of obligatory charity, but with a combined annual income of $7 trillion, 10 percent of every American breadwinner's remuneration from whatever source would amount to a tidy sum—a tidy sum, especially when one considers the taxes people would save by elimination or reduction of government's role as public philanthropist. There is no nobility in grudgingly paying taxes that find their convoluted way into the hands of the needy.

Self-reliance is another part of the price. In the depths of despair we devised emergency measures to stem the tide of economic destruction. We found ways to provide some measure of security for those beyond their productive years. We created a system that insures the integrity of savings against bank failures. We made it possible for families to live securely in homes for which they were ill-equipped to make the conventional down payment or carry a conventional mortgage. For farmers we concocted a battery of subsidies that help them stay viable. In later crises, government stepped in to protect patients and their families against the skyrocketing cost of medical care, to afford everyone a sound education, to keep them safe on the job, and to give them recourse when employment was denied them because of age, sex, race or creed. No one would argue with the good intent of such measures.

Such paternalism, however, has stripped us of the incentive to be self-reliant. Who, today, takes the time to investigate the soundness of a bank before depositing funds in it? Relatively few young people contemplate the financial implications of retirement, relying instead on employer-sponsored pension plans to supplement Social Security. Even fewer look upon home ownership as the all-consuming obligation it represents, leaving it to lenders and the government to decide if they can afford it.

No wonder the trend in American life is away from personal enterprise and to corporate dominance. Where government has come to the end of its rope, corporations have stepped in with parallel programs to assure comfortable retirement, adequate health care, help with education, and even cultural enrichment for their employees. While such assumption of responsibility by private enterprise is to be applauded, it also discourages personal risk when a secure nest awaits you at your work station. While current economics indicate a continuing drift toward ever larger business combinations, driven by an equally greater establishment of institutional investors, let us not be lulled into complacency about our individual roles in propelling our nation toward even higher goals. Nobody else can pick up the tab of self-reliance for us.

Vigilance is another item on the bill. Complacent though we are about many things, we tend to be vigilant about the wrong issues. We spy on each other, abetted by the media. We send posses into every cranny for evidence of wrongdoing only to revel in the embarrassment we have caused someone who is caught cheating on his tax return, his wife or his television ministry. Our misdirected wariness makes us as vulnerable as the voyeur watching a striptease while a pickpocket helps himself to his wallet. There are indeed threats out there. From within we must learn to fear the panderer of cheap solutions to costly problems, such as those who tell us that it takes but a simple bookkeeping sleight of hand to undo our prodigal neglect of budgetary excesses. No law, no amount of zero-based budgeting could bring our budget back into balance. Our economic boom did it for us. But it takes self-denial and constant vigilance of the type once practiced by responsible family heads who guarded the cookie jar zealously and stood firm against a trip to the movies, knowing that, popcorn and all, it impinged on the week's milk money. In larger terms it may mean doing with less; not because our country is bereft of material goods, but because we have lost the art of husbanding our resources. Our current prosperity serves only to blunt our vigilance.

From without, we must resist the vagaries of world politics. By now, we should have learned that today's friend may be tomorrow's foe, and vice versa. We showed great resolve for preparedness when the whole Communist bloc threatened us with nuclear destruction, aggression with conventional arms and subversion of our own and other friendly governments. Now that the Soviet Union is gone from the scene, we relax our vigil and proclaim the cold war to have ended in victory over tyranny. Soviet tyranny may, indeed, have sunk of its own weight and, with it, the doctrine that any degree of free enterprise is anathema. But other enemies may lie in wait for our missteps. Some wreak their venom now in the form of terrorism against which we have little defense except denunciation. A nuclear weapon in the hands of an otherwise weak nation is just as deadly, and we should watch carefully those rogue governments, especially, to whom we have transferred some of our technology.

We must understand that vigilance and suspicion are not the same. Suspicion can be instigated by evil-doers and raised to the level of hysteria, as the McCarthy era should have reminded anyone whose memory does not go back to the Salem witch hunts. Vigilance, on the other hand, is a self-directed discipline that protects us against both threats and blandishments from those whose professed intentions do not match their deeds. We need to be alert to hidden motives and, at the same time, not surrender to xenophobic panic in our dealings with exotic cultures. The blurring of this distinction led us to Vietnam and could yet embroil us in a bloodbath elsewhere. We must stand ready to take ruthless action anywhere in the world if we are truly persuaded that our self-respect is at stake, but we must make certain that our intervention is prompted by vigilance, not suspicion.

To steer this course, we must also offer intellectual honesty as part of the price we pay for national greatness. Simplistic labels are not the answer. We cannot afford, in the name of environmental protection, to forgo industrial progress and economic growth. Nor can we afford, in the name of social justice, to pervert moral, legislative and judicial principles to oil the wheel that squeaks the loudest. Nor have we time, in the name of political integrity, to look under the bed of every politician for evidence of self-seeking or to pretend that politics is a sacred calling and not a profession.

Intellectual integrity demands that we look every national problem in the face and define it, rather than classify it in a convenient category that lends itself to easy publicity and partisanship. Abortion, for example, is not a health problem, not a purely religious issue, not a matter of morality. It may be a unique issue of personal responsibility that does not fit easily into the pattern of established precepts. It has nothing to do with freedom or equal opportunity, as sloganeers would have us believe. Indeed, slogans are dangerous. They have led us into wars and demeaned us in our relations with one another.

Intellectual honesty also demands that we listen to those with whom we disagree. We must restore the fine art of debate to its former elegance by addressing the issues at hand without pinning labels on our adversaries or impugning their motives or rehearsing their past lapses in order to discredit their views. Pluralism is one of our greatest assets so long as we do not abase it by accusing others of representing special interests. All our interests are special; that is what pluralism is all about.

And when we believe we have paid the bill, we must add the tip—trust. If we are to survive as a strong nation, we must learn to trust one another. Not blind faith that breeds indignation whenever we feel betrayed, but an abiding belief that each of us is at least capable of acting responsibly. It is somewhat like the trust a drowning swimmer places in a lifeguard when there is no time to question his qualifications or the connections that got him his job. In such an emergency, blind faith is tempered by the sudden realization that someone thought well enough of the guard to place him there and that the lifesaver has nothing to gain from losing the victim, and to boot, is jeopardizing his own safety.

We must accord our public servants similar confidence. If we elect officeholders whom we have reason to mistrust, we, ourselves, are to blame for our dereliction. By and large, this rarely happens. If we find their campaign tactics indicative of untrustworthy behavior, that might be reason enough to work for their defeat. But once we have entrusted them with a mandate to lead us, we owe them an obligation of respect and support, albeit not silence when their views offend us. Once elected or appointed, they, too, have an obligation. They owe it to the electorate to work in harmony to achieve the goals they pledged to pursue. It is unconscionable for a newly installed Congress to set about thwarting and embarrassing a newly elected President of the opposite party at every turn merely to set the stage for his potential defeat four years hence. Such gamesmanship demeans the legislators and, more to the point, affronts the people who elected them to help get things done. Party politics remains an honored tradition in this country, but it also connotes a high degree of responsibility rooted in trust.

Finally, we must learn to trust ourselves. To earn that trust, we must first understand ourselves and know who we are—a people whose common cause must not become diluted by relative security and wealth. This makes it incumbent on us to understand our nation and its history, not in the context of a school lesson designed to get us through exams, but to explore its deeper meaning—what motivated our forebears to bring us to this juncture. We must understand why blood was shed first for independence and then in internecine strife that nearly destroyed the Union. We must understand whether Providence placed strong leaders at the helm at various times or whether their times exalted them. Only with this knowledge can we trust ourselves to produce leaders for our times and to give them the measured support without which we render them impotent.

We must trust our readiness to sacrifice our own worldly goods when others are in need lest we fail people who put their trust in us. We must trust our judgment in choosing, not just candidates for public office, but more emphatically the policies and course of action which these candidates espouse. We must trust ourselves to hold ourselves to the same high standards that we exact from those we delegate to represent us.

America will not self-destruct so long as we put our principles where our mouths are.

A New Beginning

One tick of the clock and we find ourselves in a new millennium. There was a momentary temptation to revise and update the pages that were written in the dusk of the twentieth century. On reflection, this seems futile in light of the theory that what was relevant some years ago is still relevant or must have been irrelevant in the first place. Moreover, it leaves us one year to ponder this dilemma since there are some who hold, not without logic, that the new century does not really begin until 2001.

But no matter. Earlier civilizations are known by the centuries in which they flourished and withered and specific years play little role in the sweep of history. The more pressing question, therefore, is whether the twenty-first century will be the one in which the great American culture will collapse. This too gives us more than a lifetime in which to make the necessary course corrections that may save this nation from extinction.

On the surface, all signs point up. Not only have we experienced an inflorescence of scientific and technological advancement. This has simplified everyday tasks and given us a glimpse of idyllic possibilities. It has cast us into the whirl of globalization as never before. Life expectancy as we enter the new millennium is longer than ever before notwithstanding the legendary Methuselah or the biblically recorded pregnancy of Sarah at 75. Diseases that once ravaged entire civilizations have been conquered even though new ones loom like storm clouds threatening an imminent downpour. Whole new sources of wealth have been devised, enriching many who dared not think of affluence only a few years ago. Yet, statistics tell us, the gap between rich and poor has widened; some say to an alarming extent.

We entered the new century as a nation at peace. But it may be only that we have surrendered some of our sovereignty to another authority that wages wars on our behalf. The dollar is strong and desirable but, at the same time, we witness national currencies being usurped by coins of a regional realm. This is not as new a concept as the proponents of the euro would have us believe. Time was when gold, measured in weight rather than paper value, was the worldwide standard. It seems we merely digressed.

The philosophy of politics, at least in the United States, has been transformed from an amalgam of intellect and leadership into a hard-nosed business in which those with the deepest pockets and most eye-catching advertising accede to positions of power. And while we may be loath to fire officeholders for missteps, we have become capable of giving them the scare of their lives much like an errant employee called sternly into the boss's office. We seem to have become enamored of the technique of disciplining public servants whenever we disagree with their policies or actions.

While paying lip service to equality and creating safety nets against the hazards of discrimination, our biases have simply found more novel outlets. Never before have Americans been more conscious of differences in color, race, age, sex and sexual orientation. Yes, the law commands us to set such distinctions aside. But in practice we do exactly the opposite in the name of compliance with these laws.

More than ever before, we have given currency to organizations that highlight the very prejudices we are determined to surmount. Name a minority (though women are hardly a minority) and you can readily find a vociferous group raising our consciousness about the injustices being visited on that minority. Entire careers, many of them lucrative, have been built on such activism. Indeed, activism has become big business.

Our sense of mercy and charity has been dulled by the rigor with which it has been institutionalized and commercialized. Giving an inconspicuous gift to someone in need no longer qualifies as a deed that merits satisfaction during inner moments nor applause when its benefits surface. The law has seen to that. With unquestionable good intent, the tax code permits donors to deduct their charities from their taxable income. Hence millions are bestowed by the very wealthy on institutions with great eclat. And for the rest of us, the fund-raising industry has concocted techniques that will extract dollars from our pockets in the most ingenious ways.

This is the age of the lure. Give your old jalopy to a certain charity, we are told, and the tax benefits will exceed the price we could garner from its sale. Pledge a major portion of your net worth to an eleemosynary organization and the resulting annuity will sustain you in later years. That at least some portion of our largess finds its way into the administrative costs of such ventures is winked at at best. True, government agencies oversee the process to unearth any excesses in profits from fund-raising but the fact remains that most giving is no longer voluntary. And still, our goodness does not suffice. Despite the currently flush state of the national treasury, or perhaps because of it, government programs akin to charity are still being written into the budget.

Perhaps this is as it should be. A combination of economic expansion as the twentieth century closed and the political pull of entitlement advocates has prodded government into constructing improved machinery for delivering well-being. And even in this endeavor there is a sense of frustration. Nothing could serve America's aging better than the Social Security system, but sober eyes have detected the moment at which the well is bound to run dry. People are living longer and more middle-aged workers are approaching the point at which they, too, should expect to collect from the fund into which they paid faithfully during their working years.

Given the anticipated budget surplus spawned by prosperity and economic expansion, there should be little dispute over how their expectations are to be met. Throw this problem into the lap of business planners and a sensible, viable plan is sure to emerge. Yet we tolerate endless debate about convoluted plans to raise the age of eligibility, transform Social Security into a vehicle for individual investment or, worst of all, let it wither and repay the victims with a politically attractive tax cut. The ultimate nature of the solution is not the issue. The issue is the vehemence with which those in charge play a spirited ballgame with what has become a sacred government obligation.

And while all this is going on, we rejoice in the delusion that our problems are being solved. The vagaries of medical care are an example that bedevils everyone except the very rich. Nobody has yet determined whose obligations our personal health really is. In an enlightened age, employers have discovered that providing for the medical expenses of their employees is a form of compensation more to be treasured than a few extra dollars in the paycheck. Concurrently, the government determined that guaranteeing health care, first for the elderly and eventually for everybody else, is the duty of the state. Toward the end of the century, private and government plans proliferated, but not all is well with the medical world.

Publicly sponsored medical programs, such as Medicare and Medicaid, are fraught with suspicion, notably among medical professionals, that the government is poking its nose under their tent. Private so-called third-party insurers exist to provide benefits while at the same time reaping profits and their motives are not in tune with those of physicians, pharmaceutical manufacturers and proprietary hospitals. And stories are legion of patients caught in the squeeze. With limits on how much can be paid out for each medical procedure, practitioners are tempted to limit the time and effort they can devote to their patients and they resist out of deference to their professional vows and ethics. Unfortunately, the overall experience of countries that have dabbled in nationalized medicine has been spotty at best.

How long will it be, in a prosperous nation like ours, before every man, woman and child, both rich and poor, need dread illness and injury only for their pain and not for their financial consequences?

Speaking of pain, how much of it is being inflicted by bullets on victims often chosen at random. When it comes to gun violence, America is surely the champion once we discount shooting wars and armed revolt. This should not be surprising when, less than two centuries ago, we blazed our way across a continent, killing the natives who stood in our path. Once established as a nation but not yet endowed with a national military, ordinary citizens became the defenders of our sovereignty as militia, enshrined in the guarantee in the Second Amendment of the right to bear arms. Such traditions die hard even when they become perverted into the use of firearms in crime.

Glorified in both history and fiction, armed predators became heroes despite their ill intentions and so did defenders of the law. Gunplay in the vaunted wild west was the rule and the main ingredient of sagas that live with us still. When all the available cattle had been rustled, robbers turned to more accessible game. First were the early railroads, victims of Jesse James and his ilk. Banks were next, unprotected by the sophisticated alarm and surveillance systems on which they now rely. As Willie Sutton put it so aptly: "That's where the money is." It would be foolish to sell such rogues as Willie short. As I came to know him rather well it became obvious that he was endowed with a superior intellect which he chose, or was forced, to apply to the only trade he had really learned. He took great pride in never having injured anyone seriously. He openly wept when someone, for wholly unrelated reasons, shot to death the man who fingered him, leading to his last arrest.

Guns in the twentieth century became a tool of the criminal trade. Small-time robbers relied on them for minor heists at liquor stores and gasoline stations. Mobsters employed them to enforce their arcane code of ethics. Worst of all, perhaps, guns have empowered the mentally deficient and deranged. In a scourge that has pervaded the turn of the century, children of a horrifyingly tender age have turned guns on other children and teachers in schools and other venues. We have reached the height of outrage and the battle has been joined. Groups representing various classes of victims have taken up the fight against gun ownership and their protests have been met with stiff resistance from the National Rifle Association and other components of what is generally called the gun lobby.

In this struggle, which can be expected to dominate political campaigns far into the future, some elementary considerations have become lost or befogged. One is the indisputable fact that guns are part of the American culture, notwithstanding that most peaceable families do not even keep a firearm in their households. But there are exceptions, all of them legal. There are the hunters who pursue their sport as a hobby with all available safeguards. Target shooters practice their art with no intention of ever aiming at a living being. Meanwhile, there are those heroic men and women who learned to kill in the wars for which the past century will be known, who have forsworn armed violence in their civilian lives but who will never forget the ugly sensation of watching an enemy human fall dead from their shots. Some, of course, have suffered emotional damage that prompts them to keep mowing down innocents in peacetime.

The so-called gun lobby is not unaware of all this. Its posture is belligerent. Consequently it fails to enlist any support from so-called law-and-order advocates and manages to alienate those who are disposed to be reasonable about firearms. It is vociferous in opposing self-evident safety devices on guns and programs that would keep guns out of the hands of children, criminals and the mentally unstable. In this melee it is easily forgotten that this pressure group represents an industry that also supplies a necessary tool in the national interest.

Gun manufacturers supply hunters, police and other law-enforcement agencies not to mention the military. On the fringe, of course, are those who produce Saturday-night specials, of no legitimate use, and their purveyors who sell underground or at ill-regulated gun shows.

It all boils down to the question of clout. That the gun lobby is a well organized pressure group, of this there is no doubt. But as we ended the twentieth century and entered the twenty-first, special-interest blocs have become an epidemic in their own right. Not a day goes by that the news fails to concern the excesses of lobbies or special-interest groups and the way they pervert the political processes which the Founding Fathers so carefully shaped to see this country through almost any problems not necessarily foreseen by the writers of the Constitution. In the process, the entire system of electing those who govern us has become warped.

Part of the dilemma may stem from the fact that office-holding has become a full-time occupation for professional politicians. Another part, not unrelated, is the ever more blurred line between the political parties, with candidates vying for the middle ground in order to attract the greatest number of votes from those who think of themselves as independents, i.e. voters without party loyalties who favor candidates who have not offended them and have not frightened them with well defined views. In an age of professional office seekers and holders, this abdication of electoral determination paves the road for those whose chief and perhaps only ambition is to live off the public budget.

Consequently, electioneering has become a quest for the largest treasury to pay for the commercialization of campaigns. Ironically, the process of vetting candidates has become murky by the evolution of state primaries which, under the guise of spreading democratic power among the voters, has emasculated the more genuine process of allowing party loyalists, at their conventions, to choose the candidates who best represent the party's beliefs and goals. Party conventions nowadays do little more than ratify the choices already ordained in the primaries.

Maligned though they may be, the smoke-filled rooms of party conventions had a virtue. The seasoned politicians who serve as delegates from all over the nation—and yes, they are dismissed as professional pols—have an innate sense of the possible. They have been conditioned to discern which candidate has the wisdom and stamina to lead the most complex nation in the world and who is electable. These qualifications do not necessarily point to the same aspirant. But their hands are tied. Under the present pernicious system, the leading candidate enters the convention floor as the inevitable nominee by virtue of his or her primary victories. This is plain wrong.

Then follows the conflict of party platforms which, with no real force, are frowardly ignored as the campaign develops. Instead, the entire race pivots on the ability to flummox an unwary electorate. But the voters themselves must bear a large portion of the blame. They want to be sold a bill of goods and they readily succumb to the blandishments of sound bites and costly television commercials.

It was not all too long ago that hordes of involved citizens flocked to the nation's major arenas to cheer their parties and to hear the candidates speak. The campaign that stands out most vividly in my mind is the first contest in 1952 between Dwight D. Eisenhower and Adlai Stevenson. It was also the adolescence of television, and these events were telecast almost completely. The addresses, notably Stevenson's, were riveting. They limned in great detail what each candidate hoped to do in the Oval Office. They lifted the veil from their personalities under the glare of the spotlight. Four years later the persuasive effect of rallies waned, possibly because we encountered the same two candidates, one of whom had already performed as president. The networks had gained some sophistication and failed to devote as much time to the campaign. More importantly, the voting public had become enamored of the living-room couch and no longer ventured out to attend such rallies.

The apparent solution, one which has survived into the new century, is the televised debate. The unforgettable encounter between Richard

Nixon and John Kennedy set the standard. But it, too, has its shortcomings. True, the candidates are on their own as they stand at their podia to answer questions posed by a panel of journalists and other political experts. But they enter the hall well briefed on whatever issue might arise in questions, a practice that follows the winner into the White House whenever he faces the media for press conferences. There is nothing really wrong with that. But because the debate format forecloses the opportunity for the debaters to address one another candidly, there is a rigidity which deprives the process of its optimum power to reveal. What a refreshing moment it was when, in 1980, in their first debate, Ronald Reagan turned to Jimmy Carter, then president, and said "Here you go again" in apparent frustration at one of Carter's remarks.

Yes, debates serve a useful function, but one must ask how much they sway the outcome. What wields most influence in today's climate is the amount of money available for television advertising and the shove given the voters by pollsters who know full well that a goodly portion of the electorate nurtures an inner desire to bet on a winner. All of this, of course, demands staggering sums of money which, surprisingly, is being proffered from various quarters with varying degrees of enthusiasm. And here the trouble really begins.

Faced with the necessity to mount costly campaigns from the moment of decision to throw one's hat into the ring, aspirants to political office assess their financial resources even more than they assess their ability to serve the public in a constructive and productive way. Given assurances that such funds can be raised, they enter the race. Denied access to the money, they contemplate ways in which they might benefit from actively endorsing someone else who does have that access. In the process, they fine-tune their stance on myriad issues that might affect voters' decisions as well as their own ability to deliver if and when they attain office. There is, of course, a temptation to be all things to all men, limited only by the degree of logic they and their counselors can apply to the positions they take. Candidates for nearly every office must also contemplate the true motives of those who support them financially and weigh the consequences of their Faustian bargains. Few, if any, are prepared to sell their souls to known forces of evil, but the human mind can easily whitewash the gray areas.

What must concern us, therefore, is the evil that campaign contributions truly imply, weighed against the highly honorable willingness to lend the most potent form of support—money—to what is almost always portrayed as a crusade for a better America, a better state or a better county or city.

In simpler times, concrete support for a favored candidate was a simpler matter. Perhaps an ardent supporter would offer his chosen candidate the use of his horse and buggy to travel through the jurisdiction in which he sought office. Others might contribute the facilities of their business or trade to provide some other sine qua non of political campaigning. Yes, some may even have donated hard cash. But there were two differences. One was that office-seeking was not fraught with exorbitant needs for cash. The other, and somewhat debatable, qualifier for public office was the fact that this pursuit attracted largely persons with considerable wealth of their own. George Washington was hardly a poor man. Lincoln, on the other hand, grew up in that legendary log cabin but had attained a modicum of wealth by the time he ran for president.

In those days, ability was equated with wealth and vice versa. Today's economy has turned such concepts upside down. But the practical effect was that the financial investment in a political campaign was usually within the reach of those who aspired to the office. Let us not be blinded by the fact that not everybody runs for the presidency, or even the governorship or the Senate. Before most hopefuls ever reach that stage, they have been elected to city or town councils, to state legislatures or a number of other positions of lesser renown and in smaller jurisdictions. For these, campaigning was economically feasible. It is when they aspire to the more exalted offices that they need to consider the question of how to finance their ambitions.

It is puzzling to watch the agony through which the nation and localities put themselves today to sort out the moral quandaries engendered by this scramble for campaign funds. Accusations of anything from law-breaking to moral depravity are floated whenever the outcome of an election displeases a segment of the public. And while the term bribery is seldom invoked, it nevertheless haunts the inquiries that ensue.

Let us make a clear distinction. Webster's defines a bribe as "money or favor given or promised to a person in a position of trust to influence his judgment or conduct." In its rawest form, a bribe is money stuffed into some official's hip pocket with the intent of getting him or her to do something illegal or against public policy, or having him look the other way when you are in the act of perpetrating an illegal act. This is a crime and, when discovered and proven in court, it deserves appropriate punishment for both parties to the bribe.

This is not what happens when benefactors lend financial support to a candidate for any office. But let us leave naivete behind and face reality. You are not going to give your hard-earned money to an office seeker who promises, if elected, to harm your livelihood or your neighborhood. You are going to give it to the candidate from whom you expect better things. It is a democratic form of self-preservation. And the higher the stakes, the more open-handed you are likely to be when standing behind the candidate or party whose success you wish to assure. It is also the democratic way to enable someone of modest means to put his or her talents and vision to productive use in governing, something that they cannot attain without financial assistance from supporters and admirers.

In today's climate, such support may require millions—certainly many thousands in smaller jurisdictions. Such sums are not disposable to the average person. They must come from organized entities with treasuries equal to the task. On the one hand these include corporations and other business enterprises. On the other, they may be labor unions or trade associations. No doubt about it, they have a palpable stake in who makes policy in their jurisdictions and they are prepared to bear the cost of getting them elected.

To be sure, individuals are solicited for contributions in the mail and by telephone but it is clear from the beginning that their donations alone are more symbolic than useful in getting the job done. Those who pledge at fund-raising dinners are more likely to be powerful in their own right or at least represent powerful entities.

Given this climate, the government, through legislation and oversight by agencies, has tried mightily to prevent excesses. And aroused by some of the doings during the 1996 presidential campaign, legislators, administrators and investigators have raised this oversight to a new art form.

In the process, a distinction has been made between "hard" and "soft" money. The first consists of contributions made directly to a candidate, to be used to defray the day-to-day costs of campaigning. The latter is money given to political parties for the perhaps-too-vague purpose of disseminating its policies and appeal to voters generally. The intended practice leaves it to the viewer or reader to associate the party's identity with that of its candidates. This means that a TV commercial or advertisement may not promote a specific candidate in space or time bought with soft money. But fertile minds have found ways of blurring the distinction and so-called issue ads sometimes have a way of insinuating the candidate into the soft-money message. This would hardly be the first time that ingenious schemers have devised ways to circumvent seemingly specific prohibitions.

Still, such suspicions cast a shadow on those election winners whose campaigns may have engaged in these practices even though their deportment in office may well be flawless. They merely enable the disappointed to satisfy their disgruntlement by implying that the person they opposed won by foul means and should not be holding office. All of this merely points up the disparity in power between the enfranchised wealthy and those whose fortunes relegate them to go with the flow.

What we tend to forget or ignore is that never in history have all people enjoyed an equal voice in the selection of their leaders. The early monarchs in recorded history took their power from the military might they were able to assemble from among their followers. The public at large never had a choice but to acquiesce in their reign. Even with the dawn of democracy, not everyone was entitled to vote. And fewer yet had a meaningful voice in the selection of potential officeholders. It was always a struggle in which economic power was bound to prevail, even when economic power was measured in terms of land and sheep. The only way for the populace to prevail was by revolutionary uprising, a concept which is clearly anathema to American thinking.

The process of accusation and investigation accomplishes little other than to inhibit the optimum performance of those who have the mandate to govern. Public funds that could house and feed the hungry are diverted to witch hunts that seldom yield much more than a shameful resignation or the destruction of a character that, in most respects, may have been worthy of leadership. Only occasionally is there a conviction and punishment.

"Turn the rascals out!" became the battle cry of the disaffected but the danger is that the rascals might be replaced by other miscreants. The happy fact is that, with rare exceptions, those who govern our cities, states and nation are an upright lot who mean well even if their decisions sometimes go awry. Moreover, we have a near-perfect mechanism for turning out such rascals as there may be. One is the periodic election process. Another is the system of jurisprudence that eventually brings outright evildoers to justice. To become preoccupied with the possibility that some dark secret lurks in every official closet is to deprive ourselves of the constructive pursuits to which we should devote our time and energies.

Not satisfied with maligning officials for their public acts, we have stooped to looking into their bedrooms as well. Having assumed that idyllic marriages go hand in hand with lofty political ideals, we think nothing of disgracing political figures for their occasional dalliances. Assignations of all kinds have been exposed among public servants as if they were unique to their profession. Some of these revelations have a tinge of the romantic; others reek of lechery. We then revel in our righteous indignation by pointing our collective finger at those who find themselves virtually forced to lie under oath. Make no mistake, lying under oath is a criminal offense, but who among us is prepared and willing to fess up to infidelity before a whole nation? Admitting it to one's wife is traumatic enough.

A notable exception was the declaration of Mayor Rudy Giuliani of New York, in the midst of his campaign for the Senate, that he was involved with a woman not his wife and, to top it off, announced plans for a legal separation from that wife before the television cameras. Ironically, it was illness, not his affection for "a very good friend," that forced him to bow out of the campaign. Ironically, too, his opponent for the Senate seat was First Lady Hillary Clinton who had her own troubles with an errant husband, a juxtaposition exploited to a fare-thee-well by the media.

Indeed, the media bear much of the blame for our prurient curiosity. They have the power to decide what constitutes the news of the day. One of their two functions is to report the news accurately and with an even hand. The other is to be advocates, surrogates for those whose individual voices are not loud enough to be heard throughout the community. But there's the rub. Advocacy assumes endorsement of that which each publication or broadcaster deems to be in the best interests of their audience. In the process, various media may come to be known as being Republican or Democrat, liberal or conservative. Some choose to think of themselves as independent, but independence itself can be misunderstood. Independent of what? We want and expect commitment from our media and commitment can never be neutral. Certainly, an editorial policy can waver between parties of the right and left so long as it is founded on a rationale. Hopefully that rationale is the public weal as they perceive it. Each publication or broadcaster will find its audience. And each audience will find and cling to the publication or broadcaster that best represents its view. To present these views and argue positions, however, does not mean to pontificate. Nor does it mean to engage in belligerence. Nothing so hardens the soil as the seeds of belligerence sown with venom. In the end, this type of advocacy turns sterile.

This means that the media need forbearance in the manner in which they practice advocacy. Digging up dirt about a perceived antagonist is no way to shape editorial policy. We have seen too much of that. In Great Britain, for example, it was unheard-of for the media to peek behind the walls of the palace until the marital agonies of the royal family spilled into the public domain of their own accord. In the United States, a sort of gentlemen's agreement kept the press from publishing what most journalists knew about the private capers of presidents and other public officials—at least until recently. And now, all bets are off. In this new environment, an officeholder's personal travails become part of the amalgam that makes him or her endorsable or subject to derision. In other words, the bedroom is now part of editorial policy.

Behind this lurks the devil of commercialism. Media sustain themselves through the size of their readership or audience. Size, in turn, influences the amount of advertising they can attract and the price they can charge for space and time. Tabloidism tends to take over, even in some of the most respectable journals. And with this vanishes the antiseptic barrier between purveyor and consumer of news. Give 'em what they want, the thinking goes, for if you don't, someone else will. Where some highly respected newspapers have preserved their norms of decency, an alternative press has found fertile ground and established itself in the fraternity of journalism.

All this, of course, in the name of free speech, one of our most treasured legacies. How much the limits of free speech have been tested can be gauged by the number of cases that travel through the court system over time.

In this sense, we can look back with great satisfaction on the survival of freedom of speech after the onslaught of the cold-war era. There was a brief time in the twentieth century when it was in peril. Communist hunters threatened many, including writers of fiction, with forced silence if their past had a tinge of left-wing sympathy or, worse, a one-time association with a communist organization. There should be no question that active support of communist causes was at best seditious and possibly treasonous. For this the law provided adequate penalties. But to muzzle creative voices for past indiscretions, especially if their leftist views were never evident in their literary output, went too far. Happily we survived this era with the First Amendment intact. But we must guard it with our lives.

*   *   *

None of the foregoing should give us great confidence that, in the year 3000, the United States of America will still be the preeminent power in the world or its most enviable society. Instead, we have slipped into a mode of self-indulgence according to which something is right simply because we are doing it. We have allowed our national principles to be perverted to serve the needs of the moment, justifying our indolence with exigencies we perceive to be urgent. When we find ourselves at wit's end about moral and temporal issues, we turn to an overloaded judicial system for answers we should be well able to supply ourselves. We have become what is possibly the most litigious culture on earth, deluding ourselves that we are parading our civilized selves by resorting to the law instead of to guns.

We have degraded our law-enforcement apparatus by casting suspicion on officers of the peace and often those who direct them. True, there are a lot of laws to be enforced; we keep piling them up at a hefty pace. We are swamped with documentary requirements for everything we do in our waking hours. We feel the government's heavy hand on our shoulders wherever we go and whatever we do. And now the government itself has become curious about how so much of our private lives should have fallen into the domain of those who seek to exploit us. Our social security numbers have become tantamount to a national identification card for just about any transaction in which we are involved.

Debt, once a liability we avoided scrupulously, has become a plastic badge of honor with which we incur ever more obligations as we career along the economic highway, unconcerned with how we plan to repay them. Consolidate your debts in one handy transaction, we are told, and you can sprint forth to spend not only your income but the paper wealth you have accumulated unheedful of risk. We have come to adulate businesses that show no profits, content with their blandishments that their gainless pursuits will expand in the years ahead. When the instrumentalities that guided us back to a path of sanity become inconvenient, we simply scrap them. Thus we now permit banking and brokerage establishments to combine forces, not having learned in the Great Depression that this was a formula for disaster. Our fear of monopoly prompted the nation to break up its oil trust but now bigger is seen as better and the disparate companies are given almost free rein to recombine.

The fact that our worship of synergy and economy of scale has rewarded us with super-everything from food stores to hospitals, blinds us to the tragedy of the small, hard-working American who catered to our individual needs and thus established himself as an invaluable asset in the community. Try to get help nowadays without pressing telephone buttons and waiting through musical minutes only to be served by a faceless operative who could care less about you. Gone is Main Street and with it the comfort and pride of the community. Ownership of our purveyors is remote, their billing addresses in the back hills where labor is cheap. Nothing defines our sense of economy better than the shopping cart. We carry home more than we need, unconcerned with how we are going to pay for it. We worship labels when once we trusted the craftsmanship of someone we actually knew personally, someone whose pride assured us of workable products and, more important, whose livelihood was inextricably linked with our patronage.

How long can we survive in this climate? We now have nearly a thousand years in which to preserve our supremacy, but some course corrections are desperately needed if the year 3000 is to find us in the exalted position we consider our birthright.

Yes, We Can

An infrequent card player, I once found myself at a table holding a hand of gin rummy. I had a decent knowledge of rummy, but here I felt incompetent. Since I last played, the game had transmuted into something I hardly recognized. To make things more interesting, for example, the ace could be played both as a one and as the card above the king. It could even be played "around the corner," i.e. a run of queen-king-ace-two-three served as a valid meld. It was no longer permissible simply to knock with cards adding up to less than ten. In order to knock, one's odd holdings could amount to no more than the open-faced card at the bottom of the pile. If that card was an ace, one was forced to wait for a perfect gin hand; knocking was not allowed.

The episode set me thinking. Was I merely out of the loop or had something gone awry with the simple pleasures of playing cards? A little of both, I suspect. Had I been a consistent participant in such games, I, too, might have welcomed some new wrinkles to make matters more exciting.

Imagine the Founding Fathers at the national gin table, observing the way the political game is played in the twenty-first century. Imagine them trying to untangle the logic behind the legislative process or to sort out the countless agencies which nowadays usurp the powers of government's three branches as ordained in the Constitution. Simple though wise men they were, the Founders would be appalled by the games being played nowadays. And probably they would be less than enthralled with the company in which they find themselves playing.

There was something innately decent about the men (hardly any women) who planted the seeds of this nation. But it would be simplistic to suggest that they were either naïve or consistently altruistic. They were driven by the shared desire to create a better life for themselves and their descendants but each had his own views of what its ingredients should be. They maneuvered and cajoled to attain their political ends within the context of the dream they jointly sought to fulfill. Their tools were primitive by today's standards and their vision limited by boundaries of the possible. So when we yearn to return to those formative days, we must do it in the context of where their vision would have led them had they been immortal. Evolution is inevitable.

In hankering for the climate in which this nation was founded we must not delude ourselves that it was a trouble-free time of unalloyed good. Rather, we would do well by examining the basic fabric of their creation and extract those fibers that would serve us well in these complex times. Today's political climate did not foster the world in which we live; quite the opposite. Our social, political and economic progress has generated the political climate. We simply cannot cram all of today's modern conveniences into the chassis to a Model-T Ford.

Yet if we are to reexamine our wayward national structure with an eye to making it serve us well for the next thousand years we cannot escape the need to refresh our inspiration with the spirit that suffused our Founding Fathers. So let us start with the basics.

In all their searching for a national structure, the Framers knew above all that they must eschew the pitfalls of the systems they had left behind. Absolute monarchy suffered from the fatal defect that power was hereditary. The English had remedied this flaw by crafting the concept of constitutional monarchy in which power was entrusted to the people represented by Parliament. The French revolution, concurrently with America's struggle for independence, took a shorter route.

It guillotined the nobility and established a republic, though it lacked staying power and succumbed to Napoleonic autocracy. And through it all, the affairs of state never really left the hands of an elite that viewed itself as ordained to lead.

If there was an emerging elite in America it had, at the very least, the virtue of self-achievement. Such wealth as there was at the beginning was hewn out of the rich but rugged land upon which the early settlers had cast their lot. As is inevitable in human evolution, some succeeded better than others. There were the rich and the poor even then, but there was a comity among them, born primarily of the struggle they had endured jointly. Wealth and wisdom were not regarded as synonymous on these shores. Above all, there was a level of trust which we would do well to recapture in our fractious times.

Out of this milieu the Founders fashioned a Constitution which has stood the test of time, if two centuries and then some can be deemed a valid test. It departed from the parliamentary concept in that it separated executive, legislative and judicial functions to provide a remarkably sound system of checks and balances. Its virtues were hailed in convincing ways. With minor variations, it was replicated by all fifty states that now form the Union. Other nations in the western hemisphere have emulated it to a remarkable degree and it has served as a model elsewhere. Perhaps most significant, there have been no challenges to the structure as a whole in the nation's history. To be sure the 14 amendments added to the Constitution, not counting the Bill of Rights and the amendments imposing and then the nullifying Prohibition, reflect both the periodic need for adjustments and a change of perception regarding the functioning of the government apparatus. None of them, however, challenged the validity of the system it established and has gloriously maintained through the years.

For all its grandeur, the Constitution remains a document with only the force accorded it by its adherents. What brought it to life was the enthusiasm with which they implemented it. For those elected to serve in its various positions of authority, it serves as an immutable guideline. What has changed is the complexion of this enthusiasm. Public office in this country began as a duty to which its holders submitted almost reluctantly. They respected the honor of being nominated and elected. They weighed the toll such duty exacted from their pursuit of a livelihood. In the end, many found greatness in their ascent to leadership, but they never regarded their stint at public service as a career, even if it turned out to be such. The stipends they were paid for their public service barely sufficed to offset their occupational sacrifices not to mention the inconveniences of the primitive travel arrangements they needed to endure. The system could ill afford the extensive staffs to which today's officeholders feel entitled. Public office was no piece of cake.

Those who felt emboldened to throw their hats into the ring did so out of sheer conviction that their point of view was more reasoned, more forward-looking than that of their opponents. In the absence of well-defined political parties they were forced to enlist popular support by means of their rhetoric and a tacit compact between them and their constituents. In some ways, they viewed political office as tantamount to a form of priesthood in which their fallibility—though not rare—was seen as a human foible, not as a rascally maneuver. Except for some notable exceptions, their honor was not impugned when they incurred disfavor with their constituencies. It was a climate to which, even in these complex times, we should once again aspire.

As long as public office remains a goal in itself, spawning lifelong careers of ever-more-exalted positions, we will not escape the problems that beset our political landscape. As a nation we cannot long afford the cost of today's political campaigns nor tolerate the animosity they generate. But how can we return to the seeming simplicity of an earlier time. Certainly it cannot be done by denying our officeholders a salary commensurate with today's economy. Time is money. Weeks and months spent in sitting legislatures demand adequate compensation. In that regard, it seems shameful that we should only now have raised the president's salary to a mere fraction of what an executive of this caliber could earn elsewhere and then congratulate ourselves on this largess. By all measures, he shoulders responsibilities that eclipse those of just about any other human on earth. Yes, he and other officeholders benefit from a variety of perquisites and exorbitant rewards after leaving office. In the early days of the republic, a public servant returned to labor on his farm or in his shop once his term of office ended. In today's environment, his labors would be eased and highly rewarded in recognition of the fame he achieved in his government role. It would be unjust to consign him or her to the career status from which they ascended to serve their city, state or nation. But for many, public office is the only career they really know after training briefly in some other profession. They have come to look upon their exalted seats in the corridors of power as an entitlement bestowed on them by their political party. It is now the party's duty to make certain that they will not go unemployed. This is an intolerable condition from which we must seek to escape to the virtues of bygone days.

An attempt has been made to remedy this flaw with the imposition of term limits in some jurisdictions, even if perhaps for the wrong reasons. Those who favor limits feel, quite sincerely, that nobody should become entrenched in a specific public office, possibly for life. True, long-time officeholders must be reelected periodically, but each victory becomes easier as their constituents become complacent. And, from the political standpoint, term limits are only a technical speed bump. If he or she must relinquish a given position after, say, two terms, it merely becomes incumbent on them to begin paving the way for the next, probably higher, office for which they will then be eligible. This does not really cut short their careers. It merely forces them to devote time to future planning that could be better spent carrying out their current duties. Just as deleterious is the effect of term limits in that they force from office talented public servants who have found a productive niche in their present jobs, whose constituents like it that way and when there is no guarantee that they will be just as effective elsewhere in government.

Term limits should be self-imposed. George Washington understood this and declined to run for a third term. Franklin Roosevelt did not and justified his voracious ambition by declaring his indispensability in times of war and depression. It must be difficult, if not heartbreaking, to concede that one has outlived one's usefulness, and probably one's youth and vigor, and step away from an exalted position—from shining fame to the obscurity of private life.

It need not come to that. By serving notice on prospective politicians that theirs is not a profession but an honor conferred upon them by trusting neighbors, we can and should vet the candidates as much for their ambitions as for their ability. The slightest whiff of political professionalism should make an office seeker suspect. He or she must present to the voters a cogent reason why they are willing to forgo other pursuits for the sacrifices—if only they were such—of serving the public. Lacking such demonstrable reasons, they should be shunned. This may be easier to say than do. But there are ways.

One shining example of sincerity is that of a widow, Carolyn McCarthy, who won a seat in the House of Representatives a few years ago. Her husband had been slain and her son severely wounded in a senseless shooting aboard a commuter train. Courageously she set out to do what she could to control the wanton use of guns in our crime-ridden nation. Her party recognized her zeal and put her on the path to the most accessible place for pursuing her mission, the lower house of Congress. To date, guns remain a menace, but she has worked tirelessly to curb their uncontrolled distribution. Allied with like-minded legislators she may yet achieve her goal. In the process, of course, she has been exposed to many other issues that warrant legislation. Her overall record as a lawmaker will eventually be judged by the voters in her district but she is determined to stick it our until her crusade has been won. When hopefully one day the country is safe from illegal firearms she may well elect to return to private life.

In a vastly different way, nobody should fault Ross Perot for pursuing the presidency in 1992. A man who had attained immense wealth in his business, he seemed convinced that there is something amiss in the way government is run. His call to arms was not unfamiliar. Many before him appealed for votes as an "outsider," i.e. as somebody not suffused in the operations of the Federal District. In current parlance this has become known as being "outside the beltway," the peripheral highway that girds the seat of the federal government. There was hardly any serious thought that Perot would ever preside over the Oval Office. Only a small percentage of the electorate accorded him their votes. Many of them, we suspect, did so out of distaste for the major party candidates rather than conviction that Perot would win or become a credible president. But why not? As they unfolded, his programs and criticisms did not have overwhelming appeal, but they proved an important point: It may be salutary to consider for office, even the presidency, someone who has something meaningful to say and the guts to prove it. In the same camp we also find Michael Forbes, the publishing heir, whose stabs at the presidency cut no deeper than a few primaries in which he fared respectably. But he, too, had a message. He proposed a flat tax to replace the cumbersome current system of income taxes. The merits of that idea will probably be debated long after Forbes has faded from the political scene.

Both Perot and Forbes made a point worth examining. Instead of pouring money into the campaigns of candidates who came closest to their points of view, thereby manipulating the parties that sponsored them, they ventured out as candidates in their own right. If you agree with them, they challenged, come out and vote for them. Though not steeped in wealth, Ralph Nader did somewhat the same thing. He offered himself for office to represent those consumers who felt themselves wronged by the purveyors of whatever goods they bought. And a goodly number of these consumers responded by contributing to his effort even though victory was nowhere in sight. A radically different constituency seemed poised to throw its weight and money behind the Rev. Jesse Jackson, probably the country's most influential advocate of the rights of African Americans. Here is a constituency with a genuine beef and few prominent spokesmen to take up their cudgels. Neither of the major political parties has championed them effectively enough to gain their long-range trust, though both have made efforts to bridge the racial gap. Given the fact that black Americans constitute a mere 12 percent of the electorate, Jackson must have been aware of the long odds of acceding to the White House, but he served his followers as a rallying point which, in the end, is what Perot, Forbes or Nader also accomplished.

However, the message is clear. If the voting public had a choice of candidates for public office at all levels who can disavow political ambition for its own sake, the profile of government could be vastly different from what it is today. Admittedly, the field would favor the wealthy. Anyone capable of sinking millions into someone else's political campaign should muster the gumption to step out and run for that office himself (or herself). Never mind that few of them have been schooled in the high art of oratory and the low tactics of muck-raking. It would surprise many of our seasoned politicians how readily a sincerity-starved public will rally behind someone whose sometimes bumbling podium performance fairly reeks of sincerity. Wendell Willkie, though a learned lawyer and articulate businessman, possessed some of that quality and in 1940 came surprisingly close to unseating a virtually invincible Franklin Roosevelt.

In the current climate, an acclaimed scientist, a persuasive writer, a successful farmer or inventor, a caring physician and many others in irrelevant careers could well rally support if only they made themselves available for public office in a variety of jurisdictions.

Our precepts of elective office are not the only ones that need rethinking if our national glory is to survive into future centuries.

Appointive roles in government are even more prone to perversion because they can be meted out by individuals and by small power centers in political parties. This affects the highest reaches of government, such as the president's cabinet, all the way to middle-level functionaries with a virtual license to rule by fiat. So let us start at the top.

As envisioned by the Founding Fathers, the president's cabinet was to serve a dual purpose. Cabinet officers, both as a group and as individuals, were to serve the chief executive as his closest advisors and, concurrently, act as the heads of specific government departments. He who appoints them, in this case the president, would seek them out among his most trusted friends for their wisdom and administrative abilities. Administration, to be sure, was a simpler task when the country was a simpler mechanism. But no matter. The American cabinet, unlike those in some foreign countries, does not make policy. Where, for example, the Israeli cabinet actually casts votes on issues—votes that are binding on the prime minister—the American cabinet voices opinions that may conflict in almost anything but their loyalty to the president. In turn, the president can pick and choose from the advice he hears in the cabinet room, knowing all the while that it is being given without ulterior motive, except to be of service. The secondary function of a cabinet member is to manage one of the government departments, looking not only to its optimum efficiency but also to its contribution toward the cohesiveness of an entire administration. It is a balancing act that imposes the need for great wisdom in a president when he assembles his cabinet.

Several factors have diluted the effectiveness of this system. First, prospective cabinet members are the exclusive choice of the president in name only. Endorsements, notably by the leaders of the party in power, serve to promote the cabinet ambitions of many whose claim on the job reflects something other than intimate friendship with the chief executive. Admittedly, they are often selected from among the managerial elite and, with faithful service, may grow into the trusted associates the president needs. It might even be said that most emerge as effective officials, both as advisors and department administrators. Their task is made easier by the fact that, with the gigantic scope of government today, they can surround themselves with excellent talent both as assistants in running their departments and in bolstering their effectiveness as advisors. Still, we have strayed far from the intimate cabinet of yesteryear.

Noteworthy is Andrew Jackson's solution to the cabinet dilemma. He would meet regularly with his real confidants and friends in the White House kitchen to discuss and resolve the issues of the day. Though never institutionalized, the so-called kitchen cabinet is believed to have served other presidents as well. Since the Jackson years, we have witnessed a substantial evolution in the role of the presidential cabinet.

There are reasons for this. With a decent amount of managerial talent, today's cabinet officer can assemble an effective staff that, in all but the highest-level policy matters, can run his department. In this complex staff, he or she can also accommodate advisors who give him or her the intellectual wherewithal to serve as a sage advisor to the president. But he or she may also discover along the way that a new breed has emerged to undercut their importance. Today's White House is teeming with somewhat unsung operatives on whom the chief executive relies even more than on his cabinet. There are, for example, a national security advisor, a trade representative, a council of economic advisors and countless others. They make their daytime home in the White House and the adjoining Executive Office Building where they are at the beck and call of the president. Where does that leave the secretaries of state, commerce or treasury? An important half of their functions has been usurped by a cadre of officials with whom they may sometimes be at odds.

We saw an example of this conflict when Richard Nixon appointed William Rogers as his first secretary of state. Rogers was a revered lawyer, a staunch party loyalist and a trusted friend of Nixon's.

Although well versed in the intricacies of international law, he was not necessarily the most experienced practitioner of foreign diplomacy.

Nor need he have been. In the wings was Dr. Henry Kissinger, an academic who had demonstrated a profound understanding of foreign policy matters through his writings and teachings. For his talents he was chosen to be national security advisor, serving the president with the day-to-day tactics needed to pursue a credible foreign policy. In time, Nixon was forced to face reality. To all intents and purposes, Kissinger had emerged as this country's foreign minister, as it were, but his contacts with foreign heads of government and their foreign ministers were frustrated by his lack of due authority to speak for the United States. The choice had to be made and, eventually, Rogers retired from his post, opening the door for Kissinger as his successor. Irrespective of whether one agrees with Kissinger's policy decisions, he distinguished himself in the post. How much he enjoyed the task of managing the State Department only he really knows. And Bill Rogers wound up with the well deserved honor of having served in the cabinet's most exalted post.

Another way in which the status of the cabinet has been undermined since the Roosevelt days is the ascension of agencies either within or outside the cabinet departments. The kindest light to be cast upon this trend is to concede that the operations of government have become so complex that each must have an office in which specific tasks are to be performed. We now speak matter-of-factly about such offices as the Environmental Protection Administration, the National Labor Relations Board, the Federal Trade Commission, the Federal Aviation Administration and countless others whose claim on authority rests in the words "federal" and "administration". Occasionally, too, we encounter ad hoc agencies that are created to cope with a critical juncture in some sector of the economy, defense, environment and the like. We must admit that the complexity of our national being might demand such agencies, including the swollen bureaucracy they inevitably engender. But we must also ask ourselves how the Founding

Fathers might have accommodated the demands of an ever-more-complex country, especially when one considers that modern technology and economics are now driving fifty—not thirteen—states?

What is wrong here is not the approach but the spirit in which it is taken. What we have seen transpire in the executive branch of the federal government is repeated to a lesser degree in all of the states and major cities. How much of what happens to us is still within our power, as people, to control and direct? It is this power that the Founders aimed to harness with their fine-tuned Constitution, but the horses have taken control of the buggy and no coachman seems to be able to stop them.

There is another precinct of public service which must be examined in light of the survival potential of the American way. It is the judiciary. Wisely, the Founders created it as a separate branch. The states and cities have followed. In biblical times judges were expected to be beyond reproach and the principle survives to this day. Perhaps the judges, with few exceptions, are beyond reproach but not necessarily the system that places them on the bench. There is room for legitimate debate over whether judges should be elected or appointed. There can be no room for debate, however, over the independence of intellect and honesty with which they fulfill their duties. The federal government attempts to achieve this goal by appointing judges and justices for life. This is to insulate them, once on the bench, from the pressures that beset all other public servants. To a large degree it does. But, human as they are, they must be expected to hew to the political considerations that led to their appointment. A president of liberal persuasion is apt to appoint liberal judges. A conservative president will do the opposite. But acceptance of a judgeship comes with no guarantees. More than once, a conservative jurist at the time of his appointment has turned liberal or vice versa. This speaks well for the independence of the judiciary. At the very least, appointment, especially for life, precludes the necessity for stooping to campaign tactics that, by their very nature, taint the aspiring judge before he even assumes the bench.

Lately we have heard much about the so-called litmus test. In scientific parlance, a litmus test requires a piece of chemically treated paper to be immersed in a liquid to determine that liquid's acidity or alkalinity. In political jargon it means that the appointing authority, e.g. the president, seeks to know in advance how a prospective judge will deal with a given issue if it is brought before him or her. Most recently the term has applied to the issue of abortion in choosing those who will make law from the bench. In effect, a pro-life president will want to know in advance that his choice for a high-court judgeship will rule against abortion rights if the issue comes before him. If not, he may hesitate to appoint him or her. What a president, nor anyone else, cannot know in advance is the subtle nature of the arguments on which the case might turn with the result that the ultimate court decision, arrived at over matters of law, may displease him. Fortunately, all responsible candidates for the presidency have disavowed the use of a litmus test, on either side of the abortion issue, in choosing judges if elected. Those with the power to appoint judges must accept the old maxim: You pays your money and you takes your chances.

There is also something to be said for the election of judges, especially in local jurisdictions. While it is impossible for most of the population to be familiar with the men and women who aspire to the federal courts or even the highest of the state courts, it is different when we select those who may someday judge us in very personal disputes. Not only are the high-court judges unfamiliar to us, but the cases they adjudicate often involve arcane principles about which we, as average citizens, have only fleeting knowledge. In a local venue, we are apt both to know the persons on the bench and to understand the civil and criminal matters that will come before them. This is as it should be. As a result, choosing judges in our own community becomes a matter of trust and respect. Optimally, those contending for a position on the local bench do not run under party labels. In some cases, the major political parties will cross-endorse, i.e. each will support the opposite party's contender in return for the same courtesy. This is done most frequently when both candidates are running for reelection after having distinguished themselves during their first terms of office.

Cross-endorsements have some merit. If there is general agreement that both candidates, though of different political stripes, have served honorably there seems to be no point in subjecting them to bruising political campaigns in order to retain the seats they justly deserve. Another, somewhat darker, danger lurks in the background, however. All too often a candidate is named not for his judicial prowess but because, as the saying goes, the party owes them something. Perhaps they have served in some other public office and come to the end of the line. They are no longer electable, too young to retire but, as lawyers, could hopefully hold their own on the bench. Or, more distastefully, they have obliged their party by serving it as sacrificial lambs. This is the term used for politicians who, out of loyalty or subservience to their party, run in an election which they and their party leaders know from the outset cannot possibly be won. Yet, the party needed to field a candidate and they offered themselves for the role. Having expended time, energy and possibly some money, they need to be rewarded. If they have the legal qualifications, what better reward to give them than to nominate them for a well-paying judgeship with a term of ten or fourteen years. Oddly enough, this practice can cut both ways. Some judges elected by this route have surprised everyone concerned by a tenure distinguished for its high judicial quality. Unfortunately, others barely get by with the aid of their law secretaries and clerks. It is certainly not a practice the Founding Fathers envisioned for the judiciary.

There is no question that, for American democracy to survive into the next millennium, we must question, review and probably revise all of the practices by which we elect and appoint those to whom we entrust the future of our cities, states and country.

But there is more to be done. We must try to reshape the very essence of our citizenry. Of course, we cannot change the people who comprise it. But we must reevaluate them in order to arrive at the inevitable conclusion that we are all equal before God and therefore equal as citizens. When Thomas Jefferson held it self-evident that all men were created equal, he spoke in the language of his times. Admittedly, women did not hold much sway outside the social arena and the word "men" was synonymous with humankind. But Jefferson, like most of his confreres, owned slaves and, in a sense, impeached his own dictum. Even his dalliance with Sally Hemings, a slave, did not raise her or her family to equal status. What, then, was the intent of his words?

In retrospect it appears that Jefferson envisioned a world, in the western hemisphere at least, that would eschew class structure as a determinant of political power. Still, that class structure persists in mutated ways to this day. We divide our society in several different ways. There are the rich and the poor, the white and those of color. No matter what euphemisms we employ, we draw lines of distinction that, according to Jefferson's words, should be anathema.

If this nation is to be a monolithic star shining bright by the end of this millennium, we must overcome, to use the words of the civil rights movement. Of course, we cannot legislate personal prejudices out of existence. They will yield to tolerance and brotherhood only when we have demonstrated that bias is self-defeating. We have made only halting progress in this respect. By various devices—- affirmative action, busing and open admission policies—we are gradually opening the doors to equal education. But we are a long way from an academia in which race, religion and ethnic background are totally irrelevant. We are beginning to see some results. The graduate mix already includes greater representation of minorities who then find their way into the mainstream of business and the professions. The armed services no longer segregate the races as they once did.

But minorities are still deprived of equal opportunity even where it is mandated by law. Truly equal housing remains a far-off goal. Those minority members who have attained professional success are finding greater acceptance in communities but we have not yet reached a point at which race is never at issue. And the faint odor of tokenism still pervades the executive corridors. The entertainment world is the lone exception, possibly because it is populated by our most liberal element.

Not all of the blame should be laid at the door of society as a whole. Those with the most liberal approach to equality are frustrated by the fact that minorities often seem to create their own stumbling blocks. It is easy to argue that prisons are populated by a disproportionate number of minority inmates, but how did they get there? Did the Almighty make them less moral or honest than the rest of us? Or have circumstances forced them into situations where living by one's wits seems the only road to a tolerable existence if, indeed, a career of crime and imprisonment can be tolerable? Deprived of hope and opportunity, they turn to life out of the mainstream. Once on the treadmill of crime, even a repentant ex-convict finds legitimate careers foreclosed. To add to the dilemma, law enforcement has turned vicious of late and the administration of justice is often seen as less than even-handed when it comes to racial distinctions.

What Jefferson and his fellow Framers probably did not foresee was the difficulty of adjusting to the end of slavery. Given their freedom, former slaves could not be expected to turn automatically into college professors or corporate executives. Except for some well intentioned organizations, there was no one to lead them by the hand into the promised land of equality. So humiliating has been their transition to freedom that some of their descendants, having attained some modicum of material success, still speak proudly of being the great-grandchildren of slaves. It is a painful confession they are impelled to make and it should be equally painful to those who must hear such reminiscences.

This country prides itself on having been founded by newcomers. Some came by choice in search of a better life. Others arrived in flight from persecution of one kind or another. And there were those who were brought here in chains against their will, to be bartered and driven, deprived of any shred of human dignity. But we are all here together, sharing the world's most sumptuous soil. It is time we recognized this as a nation.

At the same time we must be realistic. There are differences between equality and personal preferences. Many religions still prohibit marriages between persons of differing faiths. People of some nationalities still disdain unions with mates of different ethnicity. These are not dicta based solely on religious faith or ethnic purity. They are the workings of the human mind which prompt us to like or dislike certain things or people. Mental bias cannot be legislated out of existence, no matter how unjust or unwarranted it may be. What we must resolve is that each of us has a hallowed place in which to savor the bounty of our common home. Nothing gives any of us the right to deprive another human being of the same blessings we enjoy. Only when we eradicate the external manifestations of prejudice—in hiring, choosing a place to live, electing our leaders and pursuing careers— can we expect the template on which our nation was designed to sustain us into another century and millennium.

Our next concern for long-time survival must be with our sovereignty. It is a term with historic significance. The term sovereign was first applied to absolute rulers whose reign (reign being part of the word sovereignty) was indisputable. Today, we, as a nation, cherish the term as a declaration of our right to be masters of our fate.

With every treaty, with every alliance into which a nation enters, its sovereignty is diminished by some degree. The obligations of such alliances force a nation to take actions—committing troops, expending moneys, forswearing independent policies—that are not necessarily in its best interest. These obligations are part of a trade-off by which a nation hopes to gain desirable ends by ceding some of its sovereignty. It is an age-old practice, but one which we must weigh carefully. Ours is a peculiar status because of our wealth and power. In nearly every international arrangement to which we lend our support, it is the United States that must contribute the lion's share with little opportunity to demur. Thus it was that American troops bore the brunt of the fighting in wars we did not declare and in police actions to quell rebellions or incursions that did not threaten our security. Witness Korea. The Gulf War was a reverse of this. Here our national interest was clearly at stake—the threat that Iraqi conquest of Kuwait could lead to invasion of Saudi Arabia and other countries in the Middle East on which we depend for the oil that fuels our economy. But before we could defend our interest we were obligated to obtain the consent of the United Nations. In the end, it was American military forces that planned and executed the operation, fortunately without loss of life, with only token help form those whose consent we first needed in order to take action.

Abhorrent as war of any sort may be, there is something majestic in the right of a nation to declare war. The act was never taken lightly. Yet, December 8, 1941, the day after Pearl Harbor, was the last time the United States declared war on anyone. (The subsequent declaration of war against Germany and Italy was merely a corollary necessitated by the Axis by which our enemies united against us). The modern technology of warfare may well make it impossible for the Congress to deliberate declarations of war in the future. Pearl Harbor, for all it swiftness and surprise, was only a precursor of the rapid deployment of missiles against us that can come virtually from any quarter nowadays.

At the same time, we have fallen into the dangerous habit of euphemizing war. Police action and peace-keeping operations are but two expressions devised to shield us from the reality that we are at war somewhere in the world. Vietnam, to be sure, was a war—in effect an American war—but our entry into it was so gradual that the severity of it eluded us until it was too late. Let us not fool ourselves if we want to survive the millennium. Do we really want to go to war—for that is what shooting and bombing is—to prevent Hutu and Tutsi or Serbs and Croatians from slaughtering each other as they have been wont to do for ages? Do we really need to expose American soldiers to mortal danger in order to establish governments to our liking in countries whose affairs of state have always been unsettled? Unless, in some way, possibly indirect way, those regimes pose a threat to our safety or economic health, we should revert to the time-honored practice of declaring wars only when absolutely necessary. We now use a subterfuge. Congress is no longer asked to declare war. Instead Congress need only appropriate the funds necessary to pursue a specific military action and the killing can begin.

The power to declare war, by whatever cognomen is in fashion, has been ceded to supranational organizations, such as the United Nations, which was formed precisely to prevent war, or to NATO which was designed to organize a common defense in the event of attack against one or all of its members. Are we really still a sovereign nation?

Our deference to such supranationals is well intentioned but misdirected. Following the bloody experience of World War I, the victorious belligerents formed the League of Nations as a vehicle for preventing a world conflict from ever recurring. The United States declined eventually to join the League, largely because it was recognized at the time that we would need to cede some of our sovereignty in the process. The League withered on the vine, partly because there were no wars to prevent. Its members had not yet invented police actions, peace-keeping missions and the wide-spread do-gooder programs that are now part and parcel of international organizations. The abstinence of the United States and the lack of its monetary support may have added nails to the League's coffin.

Once again, after World War II (which the old League of Nations might not have been able to avert in any case given Hitler's madness) another attempt was made with the creation of the United Nations. We will never know whether the U.N. actually prevented the cold war from turning hot. We do know that, at the height of the east-west conflict, the U.N. was beset with a shoe-thumping disruption by the Soviet leader, though, in all fairness, we must concede that the specter of a world war is more remote now than ever. In the process, of course, each of the member nations relinquished a fraction of its sovereignty for a good cause.

But sovereignty may be on its way out. We see it happening in Europe and we must regard the trend with a leery eye no matter now beneficent its goals. What began as a common market to promote free trade among western European nations matured into the European Community. This implies more than a trading arrangement. It suggests strongly that nominally independent countries must accede to economic strictures not of their own making. To solidify this bond, they created a pan-European currency, the euro, to eventually supplant their own monetary systems. With control over one of the basic components of national identity surrendered, how long can it be before the members of the European Community will have to cede their governmental independence as well? And all this on a continent where nearly every national border, often a boundary of natural phenomena, contains populations with distinct ethnic, moral and judicial precepts. Defenders of this trend point to the heightened prospect for peace on a continent torn by too many wars in the past. Its opponents raise the specter of a United States of Europe in which a multi-national, multi-ethnic government rules the continent from a central capital indigenous to only one of its peoples. Shades of the Holy Roman Empire.

We must guard against being engulfed by this maelstrom. In an ironic sense, the process should not seem alien to us. Here, fifty states have subsumed some of their sovereignty to one national government and accepted a single currency and it has worked remarkably well for more than two centuries. But there is a difference. No one state is the province of a single ethnic group. The power entrusted to the individual states was clearly defined in the Constitution and remains lodged there within the limits imposed by this compact. As a result the United States has historically regarded itself as a single sovereign power. The bottom line is: We are still one sovereign union. When that principle was challenged we fought a civil war to preserve it. We must guard and preserve our sovereignty if we are to survive.

*   *   *

History is awash in empires, really civilizations, that flourished and vanished. Each enjoyed its centuries on center stage until its time had come to be relegated to the history books. Various failings precipitated their decline. A lost war. Ineffectual leadership. Disintegration of the popular will to excel. But most of all it was their inability to adhere to the principles that defined their sovereignty in the first place. Times do change. Failure or refusal to adapt can be destructive, but not as destructive as the headlong rush to conform with an alien template that is inconsistent with the national ethos. If we, as a nation—a unique civilization grown out of an amalgam of peoples—allow ourselves to be changed by the world around us we, too, will meet the same fate. We cannot let this happen. Here, then, are some necessary precautions:

We must begin by taking a hard look at the basic premise that guided the creation of the Constitution, as sage a document as may have ever been written by mortals. We must take everything it says at face value. We must eschew the temptation to stretch it, warp it to suit concerns of the moment, or to over-interpret it. The Framers meant what they said, and their judgment was superb. They perceived the dangers of changing the Constitution and weighted it with a cumbersome process for amending it. Only on the rarest occasion has that process been employed for frivolous reasons. But there are other ways of polluting the noble content of that document.

One of these is derivative reasoning. One example that comes quickly to mind is the prohibition, in the First Amendment, against imposition of a state religion. A noble precept, it has fallen victim to a slogan the Framers never envisioned —separation of church and state. True, this is what was meant by precluding a national religion. The government should have no right to dictate how people worship or whether they believe in God at all. But to suggest that no aspect of governing this country may ever touch on the boundaries of religion is absurd. In God We Trust is a motto that is part of our coinage, perhaps to the chagrin of atheists. A clergyman opens every session of Congress and the military services provide chaplains for every unit. And yet there are countless debates and litigations that tug at the fringes of the Constitutional taboo. Whether it be prayer in public schools or a Christmas tree on city hall steps, these are minutiae that demean the grand scheme of the Constitution and waste untold funds and energy.

The simple fact is that this country is populated by adherents of so many religious sects that it would be mathematically impossible to establish a state religion promulgated by any one of them. True, the majority of Americans are Christians but their diversity is so great as to render any one of them powerless to entrench theirs as the ruling religion of the land. Whether this was evident even in the days of the Founding Fathers is debatable, but their prescience is one of their great gifts to us. When it comes down to present reality, waving the banner of separation of church and state is either empty posturing or a cover for other motives. Let us be alert to this.

The temptation to warp the basic law is another reason for caution. Needless to say, abortion was not on the Founders' minds in light of their era, but it illustrates the point. The justifiable controversy between right to life and freedom of choice is one that must be resolved in the hearts and minds of those faced personally with the problem. Since freedom of religion reigns under the Constitution, it is futile to bind any religion to a national precept, by legislation or otherwise. There is no Constitutional issue when activists resort to violence in order to enforce their point of view. There are criminal laws against such violence and they are consistent with the Constitution. Nor is it an issue of free speech. Everyone has a right to express his or her views on such issues as abortion, always conscious of the right of the opposition to demur.

In the same context, the right of free speech has become an issue in its own right. While few would challenge this right, there are many who strive mightily to defend it when it is not under attack. Pornography is a case in point. Nobody ever suggested that lewdness in speech, print or drama is not offensive to some. Those offended have remedies, the best of which is to turn away from it. Without customers, pornography will not long pervade the media. But to argue at length in the courts whether suppression of lewdness infringes on the right of free speech is tantamount to starving a naughty child rather than to educate it. Processes such as these pervert the intended nature of the courts whose primary function it is to adjudicate palpable disputes, with the highest courts called upon to resolve those issues on which lower benches disagree or have become frustrated in making a satisfactory determination. To the extent that the judiciary does, indeed, make law, let it be law that is germane to their basic function—the preservation of the Constitution.

But courts are not, and should not be, the venue where laws are made. That role redounds to the Congress and in a similar way to the state legislatures, city councils and village boards. Here again, the Framers laid out a sensible plan. They charged the Congress with the duty to legislate in order to make the wheels of government turn smoothly, to appropriate the necessary funds for doing so and to outlaw any activities deemed injurious to the nation. This role has been similarly assigned to state and local legislative bodies. But it has been perverted.

To arrive at the most effective legislation, Congress and other legislatures must inquire of the ablest minds about the best route to the desired result. Hearings of this sort are very much in order. But it is a perversion of this process to turn such hearings into inquisitions intended for, or resulting in, the vilification of individuals or groups or to sleuth for incidences of wrongdoing. The McCarthy hearings of the 1950's were the outrage that should have turned us away from this practice, but it surfaces periodically and, to our shame, meets with considerable eclat in the media and among the vindictive among us.

Another legislative mandate is to provide the nation, and the various jurisdictions within it, with workable budgets. It is inescapable that the demands of modern times have rendered budgets so complex that the process is beyond simplification. But to elevate it to warfare among factions and against a White House of opposite persuasion is to frustrate the creation of a workable budget. Is there room for a bit of horse-trading and pork-barrel provisions? There probably always will be. The best way to limit them is to reconstitute our national and state legislatures to consist of something other than professional politicians. After all, pork-barrel budgeting is intended to help a legislator perpetuate his tenure in office. The Founding Fathers may not have anticipated the tenacity of future leaders in clinging to their exalted posts. We must return to the concept of public office as a path undertaken as a civic duty, perhaps at some personal sacrifice.

But let us not be naïve. The prestige and power of public office are intoxicating. We must learn to distinguish between those who have succumbed to this addiction and those others who have decided simply to feed at the public trough as a career choice. While both can be detrimental to the survival of our national grandeur, the unabashed professionals care least about national survival and merely want to perpetuate their own rides in the political arena. Such ambitions have led to the destruction of ancient empires, only then the destructive force consisted not so much of office-holders as of warriors for whom power was a goal in itself. How do we make such distinctions in our times—in our national structure of two major political parties?

One way is to scan the history of candidates for tell-tale signs. Not their advertised devotion to family and community nor their cookie-cutter professions of past achievements. Rather, to be effective voters, we should find out how faithfully they have attended and participated in their local political clubs awaiting their first nomination or appointment to public office as a reward. Once installed, did they ever return to the private sector voluntarily rather than by unwished-for defeat at the polls? Or was their ascension to high office a series of promotions predicated on their ability to get votes? One tell-tale sign of professionalism is the "storage" as it were of a defeated officeholder in an appointive job until he or she can be readied for another try at the ballot box. A political party will not let its faithful-—its stock-in-trade—- go unemployed for very long. While in office, public figures must be closely observed in order to determine whether they appear to compromise principle for political expediency. Adherence to the platform of their party is acceptable, but blind submission to its dictates must be suspect. In other words, we must be vigilant in our selection of leaders and this is not an easy task. It means attendance at political and public events, not just a handshake at the commuter railroad station. It means reading campaign literature for subtle signals, not just tossing it into the paper basket.

Having thrived under the two-party system, we should put the parties to work for us, as they so loudly proclaim to be doing. Just as former alcoholics are especially gifted in leading others back to sobriety, so professional politicians have the talent for vetting avowed office-seekers for their ability to serve. Party conventions serve this purpose, or at least they once did. But this function has been undercut by the proliferation of primaries which emasculate and subvert the convention as an instrumentality of choice. This is especially true of our presidential primaries. By the time the conventions convene, their parties' nominees are all but predetermined, bound as they are by the rules that make delegates subservient to primary results in their respective states. In effect, what we have in November differs little from the run-off elections by which some countries choose their leaders, i.e. a contest between the two front-runners.

As professional politicians, to whom we are already married and whom we are reluctant to divorce, convention delegates should have an opportunity to exercise their judgment of who, among all the contenders, is best able to engage the electorate's imagination and support and, even more important, who is morally, intellectually and administratively best able to govern the nation or state for the next four years. Has it always worked? Most of the time it has, even though it did not always produce the historic figures we wish our presidents to be. It can be argued that of the forty-two presidents who have led this nation, only a handful, perhaps a half dozen, have been great figures and the rest mediocrities. You take your choice of which they were; your judgment is as valid as anyone else's. (In this context, mediocrity must be defined by the high plane on which each president functions. No ordinary mortal attains this level of distinction just by being an ordinary mortal.) And of those "great" ones, how many had greatness thrust upon them by the eras in which they served and how many made their time memorable by their governance? But no matter. Our strength as a nation derives from our collective wisdom and dedication to all things public. The leaders we elect derive their strength from our support and guidance and this is at it should be if we are to survive as a great power. Many of history's "greatest" leaders were dictators and we know what happened to their domains.

Having vouchsafed the character of our nation's leaders we must consider America's position in the world. We stand alone as this planet's richest and most powerful country. While this may impose some moral obligations on us, it does not anoint us as the world's policeman, peacekeeper or guardian. We live in a world where national boundaries are just that—geographic lines of demarcation. They are breached by internet communications and virtually unimpeded commerce. Through modern communications we, or rather our citizens, share in scientific progress, commercial enterprise and artistic development almost as if these borders did not exist. This leads to the temptation to ignore national boundaries because we also have the mechanisms for involving ourselves in the affairs of most other nations, except the few rogue states with which we deign not to have intercourse. But even those proscriptions can be breached in ways that usually involve other countries that do not subscribe to them. Hence, it is forbidden to buy or smoke Cuban cigars in America, but Americans have access to them when visiting a country that has no such embargo. We can and do use foreign soil to warehouse money and licenses to evade American taxes or regulations. While this may be a repugnant practice, it illustrates the degree to which national boundaries threaten to become meaningless unless we discipline ourselves, perhaps at some cost, to abstain from this type of exploitation. To make matters worse, the affected countries welcome the practice because it gives them access to funds they might never enjoy otherwise.

In effect, we are skating on thin ice when it comes to preserving our sovereignty and our primacy in this shrinking world. It would be unrealistic to suggest that interdependence is not a way of life. But even in this climate we must strive to preserve our hard-won supremacy. We won it in two world wars and saved weaker nations from conquest. We won it again by holding fast against the communist threat spearheaded by the Soviet Union and proving, in the final analysis, that our system has staying power. We win it virtually every day by inventing, producing and harvesting the world's finest crop of products and natural goods. And we defend it by our readiness to subdue the challenges of those who would bring us down.

More than once we rose to that challenge since the end of World War II and only once did we fail to succeed. When the communist threat gave us fear that free nations would topple like dominoes, we engaged in grim battles in Korea and Vietnam, neither of which we won outright. In Korea, the peninsula remained divided between a communist north and a democratic south, with a heavily armed dividing line at Panmunjom still in place fifty years later. In Vietnam we cannot remotely claim victory although, when all is said and done, southeast Asia did not fall like dominoes as we had feared when we embarked on that misadventure. Indeed, we have learned to accept the reality that deeply entrenched communist regimes still rule mainland China, North Korea and Cuba. We are only slowly coming around to reconciling ourselves to the prospect that their aging leaders and the lure of world commerce will force communism to yield to the advantage of free economics. Patience is indeed a virtue.

But we must learn lessons from all this. Despite our undisputed power and influence, it is not for us to dictate the nature of foreign countries' internal policies. We may be appalled by their treatment of minorities, dissidents or women. But intervention gains us little except animosity from those who regard their perverse practices as a sort of birthright. And yet we have been goaded several times into throwing our weight, by diplomacy or even armed intervention, behind the efforts of those who want to change the status quo in their own countries. Worse, we yield to the obligations imposed on us by supranational organizations when our wisest course of action would be to mind our own business. Unless our own national interests are directly threatened we must learn to either do business with or abstain from trading with those whose practices and policies we find repugnant.

To do otherwise is to invite accusations of empire. We do not wish to rule the world nor can we afford to. And historically it was after empires reached the zeniths of their power that they began to crumble. Let us not follow their examples.

Democracy as we know it is a wonderful thing. But is it fungible or exportable? A sage friend raised that question nearly forty years ago when Patrice Lumumba seized power in Zaire, once the Belgian Congo. Alarmed by the mischief he might wreak, we bent every effort to upend his regime and, hopefully, install democracy in that far-off country. "Do you really believe," my friend asked, "that you could have spring primaries and general elections as we know them in that jungle?" The answer was obvious. Lumumba sank of his own weight.

The thing to remember is that all regimes worldwide are based on the cultures from which they sprang. There were monarchs and tribal chieftains. There were revolutions and religious fundamentalists. Our own democracy, by God's grace, has its roots in a culture of immigrants who thirsted for the freedoms that characterize our system of government. That shoe simply does not fit all just because it fits us. We experimented with exporting our brand of liberty when we sent troops to Haiti to oust a regime of questionable legitimacy and to restore an elected president to power, and how we failed. With all but a few of our military units remaining to police the turf, disorder bordering on anarchy has returned to that hapless island nation.

Nor do we wish to become an empire whose demise becomes just a matter of time. Watching even the British empire disintegrate, albeit under peaceful and controlled conditions, we should understand that the costs of empire are such as to render it self-destructive. Moreover, our national temperament does not tolerate the concept of domination over other lands and people. It simply is not in our blood. We know that there is such a thing as spreading ourselves too thin.

Instead we should husband our power in order to create a society with enough durability to do what no other has ever achieved—survival for millennia as a cohesive nation that will dominate the world in a unique way. Rather than foster an empire by conquest, we must set an example that will impel other cultures to emulate ours. Only in this way will the world gravitate toward us as the nucleus of the "One World" once envisioned by Wendell Willkie. This is the kind of empire a shrinking world will embrace.

To do this, we must strengthen the social fabric of our nation. In this utopia there can be no poverty, no prejudice and no strife. Easier said than done, perhaps, but attainable. To eradicate poverty we cannot rely on government programs to bolster the disadvantaged. Only private enterprise with rampant imagination, achievable goals and an open door to all who want to contribute their talents, elementary as they may be, can attain this objective. It is futile for government to tax the private sector and then pass the money along to those who can and should work. With the wheels of industry humming and consumers spending—along with some judicious saving—there can be jobs for all who want to work. To use taxation as a vehicle for redistributing wealth is pure folly. Taxation should serve only one purpose, which is to keep the machinery of government oiled.

There cannot be and never will be total equality. Those with the most fertile imagination, those dedicated to the ethic of hard work and a willingness to take sensible risks will always fare better than those with limited vision or ability. And, yes, there are those who inherited their status. To take away what their forebears amassed is not only unfair but counterproductive. Human greed being what it is, those born into wealth will usually strive to increase their fortunes and, in the process, create new enterprises and employment. With the prospect of seeing their affluence diminished by taxation, they will eschew risk and thereby diminish the opportunity they could create for others. Ours is a sturdy society and we must nurture it, not tamper with it.

The opportunities we create must be open to everyone. While we can never fulfill the wish for equal opportunity—a slogan better suited to rhetoric than reality—we must create a climate in which the determinants are revised to accommodate the facts of life. People are not endowed with equal degrees of intelligence, ambition or muscular strength. Not everyone can succeed in the same degree. But, if our society is to grow and prosper, we cannot acknowledge differences of race, ethnic background, religion or sexual orientation. It is we, as a people, who must level the playing field ourselves. Government cannot and should not do it, except by broad statutory and common law that outlaws discrimination. Orators cannot and should not do it because their outbursts serve only to alienate those whom they presume to address. Educators can and must do it because they can reach into the minds of those anxious and willing to learn. But this takes time.

We must have to await another generation or two before we can attain a populace that no longer regards personal background as an indicator of what one group or another can contribute to the general weal. We should be confident that there will come a time when obvious physical appearance, notably skin color and manner of speech, will be taken for granted as readily as we accept differences in architecture or fashions. Differences come with the territory and we must resolve to accept them with equanimity.

In order to assure ourselves of perpetuity as a nation and society, we must forswear strife. There is a critical difference between disagreement and strife. Disagreement serves as a fertilizer for the soil in which our national strength must grow. Our best minds have an obligation to debate and inquire for the most efficacious route to national success. Lesser minds, too, must have their say in the way we progress. It is the healthy outpouring of opinion that paves the road to achievement.

Strife is another thing. Civilized folk understand—or they must be made to understand—that acrimony is not persuasive, that it acts as a brake on our journey to greatness. It is one thing to defend one's beliefs, quite another to threaten violence or harm against those who disagree. As long as there is poverty and prejudice, however, strife cannot be extinguished. Frustrated in their efforts to participate in the mainstream of society, the disadvantaged are tempted to fight for their rights. Those threatened by their belligerence vow to fight back in what they regard as self-defense. No team beset by internal strife has ever won a game. We must begin to think of ourselves as a team, pursuing a common goal.

Crime is a form of strife—one that often affects innocent bystanders. To be sure, there are some with warped minds who believe themselves to be best able to attain objectives, large and petty, by engaging in crime.

Punishment for criminal behavior is as old as civilization itself. But too much of current crime stems from disenfranchisement. Poverty alone does not spawn it; hopelessness does. In a society cleansed of prejudice, crime will no longer pay.

At the same time, we must learn to curb our instinct to become bellicose when our opinions are not heeded. Name-calling in political campaigns and defamation of those who disagree with us leads to a form of strife that may not always be violent but is always destructive of our self-respect as a nation. Open demonstrations are a subtler form of strife. That they may become violent is borne out by the presence of police whenever a public demonstration is held. More than just holding the potential for violence, demonstrations also send the wrong message to the world. We live in a world where mobs erupt and have been known to overthrow regimes. The fact that ours are gatherings controlled by permits and supervised by usually responsible leaders does not prevent them from being viewed abroad as revolutionary symptoms. Our friends view them with concern, our enemies with glee. In the end they accomplish little except to elevate their causes to the headlines. There are better ways to express our factional concerns under the guarantee of free speech.

*   *   *

In many ways we have yet to attain the full glory of what we envision as our permanent predominance in the world. No, America is not likely to self-destruct anytime soon, but the pitfalls are always there. We have the will and the competence to avoid them. We have the resources, both material and intellectual, to blaze a trail to eternal glory. We have the structure of government to make it feasible. What we need to enhance is the discipline with which we conduct ourselves as citizens of a shrinking world. We have that fragile self-respect which must accompany us in everything we do and which we must nurture by honoring our accomplishments as a nation of one people. We have work to do.

About the Author

For more than fifty years, Walter H. Stern has been an involved observer of the American scene from a number of pivotal vantage pints. His hands-on experience includes close observation of law enforcement and criminal justice, activity in political campaigns and in public office, executive functions in the corporate world and as commentator on matters of energy and environment.

During thirteen years on the staff of *The New York Times*, he covered political campaigns, criminal and civil court proceedings as well as the housing and real estate scene. In the public relations business, he represented a broad spectrum of industries, societal causes and political campaigns. As a corporate executive, he worked closely with the financial community and charitable organizations. His writing on energy and environmental issues, among others, appeared widely as Op-Ed page commentaries published by Mobil Corporation, from which he retired in 1987.

His political interest began in 1940, when he was a high-school senior and not yet a U.S. citizen, by offering menial services to local organizations during the Willkie presidential campaign. Through his association with a public relations firm, he provided counsel to several municipal and legislative campaigns and later served as Commissioner of Assessment and Taxation of the City of Glen Cove, where he resided at the time.

Mr. Stern was born in 1924 in Frankfurt am Main, Germany, and immigrated to the United States in 1936. A graduate of New York University, he is the author of previous books about business and real estate.